RACE and MIXED RACE

RACE and MIXED RACE

Naomi Zack

Temple University Press

Philadelphia

Temple University Press, Philadelphia 19122
Copyright © 1993 by Temple University. All rights reserved
Published 1993
Printed in the United States of America

Library of Congress Cataloging-in-Publication Data
Zack, Naomi, 1944–
Race and mixed race / Naomi Zack.
p.   cm.
Includes bibliographical references and index.
ISBN 1-56639-064-8 (alk. paper)
1. United States—Race relations.   2. Racism—United States.
3. Racially mixed people—United States.   4. Family—United States.
I. Title.
E185.615.Z33   1993
305.8'00973—dc20   92-44252

Epigraph from a letter to Friedrich Treitschke (1821),
in Emily Anderson, trans. and ed., *The Letters of Beethoven*
(London: Macmillan, 1961), no. 1068.

The work is dedicated to my sons,
Alexander and Bradford

Let us begin with the primary original causes of all things, how something came about, wherefore and why it came about *in that particular way* and because it is, why something is *what it is*, why something cannot be exactly so!!! Here, dear friend, we have reached the ticklish point which my delicacy forbids me to reveal to you at once. *All that we can say is*: it cannot be.
—Ludwig van Beethoven

Contents

Preface and
Acknowledgments

I was born in Brooklyn in 1944. My mother was a single parent and I was an only child. She was an artist, the youngest of seven children in an immigrant family of Russian Jews who came here from Vilna in 1903.

I grew up on the Lower East Side and in Greenwich Village, except for three years in Westchester County. I majored in Psychology and, later, Philosophy at New York University, and I was a student in the Department of Philosophy of the Graduate Faculties of Columbia University. My dissertation was titled *The Epistemology of C. I. Lewis*, and I was awarded the Ph.D. in 1970. I then left academia and Philosophy and did not return until 1990.

I was a conscientious student, slightly out of phase with my peers but well recognized by my teachers. During my student years, race was not an issue for me: I did not have to identify myself racially on any forms, and I do not remember any official person in the New York City public school system, in college, or in graduate school asking me what race I was. If racial identification had been required, I would have identified myself as my mother had brought me up to do: I was "Jewish." My mother was not observant but she strongly knew herself to be a Jew.

My mother had a close friend while I was growing up who was married to someone else. He regularly drank too much and was rarely sober when he visited my mother. He seemed to be indifferent to children although—or because—he and his wife had ten. He rarely spoke to me. He faded out of our lives when I was twelve. When I was sixteen I found out that he had been my father.

My father's father had been born a slave in Virginia, and he was six years old at the close of the Civil War. My father's mother was from the Oklahoma-area Sioux. When I was sixteen I thought of my father as a Negro. During most of my adult life I thought of him as black. Now I think of him as mixed race.

I have always lived in racial ambiguity. I have resisted identification as black, Jewish (if Jews are a race), or white. My preference has been for people to accept me "as I am." They have so accepted me for the most part, in school, in nonacademic projects in business and the arts, through marriages and divorces, in friendship, and in family life. I sometimes felt that it was wrong of me to have the father I did, and I knew that I was wrong to feel that way. My racial ambiguity did not make me happy, but it afforded me a degree of freedom. Race did not seem to be preeminent in my life—until 1990 when I returned to academia.

Between 1970 and 1990, academia had become racialized. Now race is a big issue. Students, teachers, staff, and job candidates are all classified racially. Still there is little evidence that this has equalized educational opportunities for non-whites in general; along with demands for greater "diversity" on campus have come academic reflections of the racist backlash against increased civil rights for African Americans in the culture at large. Meanwhile, the old universalist ideals of equality through education have withered into a defense against the kinds of emancipation that universalism was once thought to guarantee.

I taught on an adjunct basis for three semesters, beginning with the spring term of 1990. During that time, I became interested in new philosophical subjects, in Feminism, the Philosophy of Pedagogy, and, Racial Theory. These subjects would not have been possible during my graduate school years, although they are still improbable in many traditional departments of philosophy. An autobiographical paper in Racial Theory was among my application materials for a full-time job.[1] In March 1991, I accepted a tenure-track position in the Department of Philosophy through a university (minority) affirmative action recruitment program called Target of Opportunity (TOP) at the University of Albany of the State University of New York. I chose this job over a West Coast "regular" opportunity, in part because I thought it would provide an existential occasion for me to address racial issues philosophically. Out of ten thousand academic philosophers in the United States, only seventy-five are "of African descent," a number that is further reduced by the category of female gender. To be publicly and officially "in that number" would sharpen anybody's wits along racial lines.[2] For me, the result has been this book.

If I have been ambiguous about race in my life, I am ambivalent about it philosophically. Philosophically, I am ambivalent between constructing a theoretical identity of mixed race, for which there is no place in the American biracial system, and, on grounds of science and good faith, rejecting all forms of racial identity. This philosophical ambivalence cannot be resolved, but I think it holds more truth than my lived ambiguity. If the truth does not always set one free, it can at least wake one up. In this case, I have awakened from a dream into a nightmare. But, for reasons I cannot fully explain, I think I am better off for it.

I began writing the manuscript during the winter of 1991, completed a first draft in August 1991, and wrote and edited for a year after. I received important encouragement and useful criticism over various drafts, and I am particularly grateful to the following people for written comments and discussion about these drafts: Berel Lang, Felman Davis, Linda Nicholson, and Ed D'Angelo. I also benefited from conversation with Leonard Harris, Bill Lawson, Claudette Jones, Claudia Murphy, Lillian Williams, and Norma Riccucci.

I have a special debt to Gloria DeSole, director of affirmative action at the University at Albany, for her support since the first draft of the manuscript.

As the publisher's outside reviewer, Lawrence Thomas contributed insightful comments that led to several adjustments of my conclusions. For example, I added the discussion of folk concepts of mixed-race identity at the end of Chapter 13.

I am respectfully grateful to H. Patrick Swygert, president of the University at Albany, for his accessibility to beginning faculty and the interest he has expressed in my progress with this manuscript.

I am very fortunate to have Jane Cullen of Temple University Press as an editor. She is forthright, efficient, judicious, and her standards of professionalism and clarity have informed many aspects of this book. Thanks also to Jennifer French, production editor at this press, for meticulous work, efficient dispatch, and great courtesy.

Joanna Lee Mullins, freelance copy editor, took extraordinary care with the manuscript beyond the call of duty.

Linda Dayly was a patient assistant in my word processing of the manuscript. Thomas Reynolds has been a painstaking and philosophically attentive proofreader, on my end.

Gina Gaetano, who, based on her own life and work experience, understands my analyses of race in the United States, was always willing to lend an ear to my accounts of this project's development.

I do not think I would have been able to conceptualize the issues raised herein if, before I returned to academia, Jack Abbott had not spent a year or two trying to help me rewrite a manuscript about my childhood. That blighted autobiography was part of the necessary "therapy" before this philosophy, and it also made me stronger as a writer.

As a mother of teenage sons, I have had the necessary long, quiet time to devote to my scholarship overall, because my former husbands Jerry Erdmann and Tom Mahon are full-time fathers. And, of course the main "right" reason to undertake a work of this nature is the hope that the next generation, of everyone's children, will suffer less from matters of race.

So I do not lack for people with whom to share any praise. But as these things go, the blame is all mine. And rightly so. This book is my gratuitous contribution to several traditions—the world did not ask for it.

N.Z.

March 1, 1993
University at Albany, State University of New York

Note on Quotation Marks and Italics

A note on my use of quotation marks is probably in order here. Double quotes are used to refer to words and single quotes are used to refer to terms and concepts. When terms and concepts are used for the first time, they are italicized. Double quotes are also used as 'scare quotes' and italics are used for emphasis and for unusual foreign words. While these rules may not be standard practice, they serve the requirements of philosophic discussion (which is not to say that all philosophers would agree with them).

I

THE
EXISTENTIAL
ANALYSIS

1

Introduction: Summary, Method, and Structure

t has been acknowledged for a long time that there are racial problems concerning black people and white people in the United States. And there has been a shifting spectrum of moral, political, social, and legal argument about how whites ought to treat blacks, as well as a less visible but equally unstable spectrum of views about how blacks ought to react to whites. This book is not about either one of those spectra.

This book is about the concepts that result in the categorizations or designations of American people as black or white. The focus is specifically on American categories of racial inheritance and identification for several reasons: American racial existence is distinct from that of other societies; American issues of race have always been problematic; American racial issues are important because they affect millions of people and because they affect those people importantly as individuals. I have spent most of my life in American culture, and my own genealogy is bound up in its history in ways that yield a depth of understanding that would be difficult, if not impossible, to reach about some other society.

The subject herein is further limited to black and white American racial designations. This is regrettable because much remains to be analyzed about the racial designations of Asian Americans, Native Americans, Hispanic Americans, and Semitic Americans. However, this should be read as a limitation of academic specialization only.

The general thesis of this book is that black and white racial designations are themselves racist because the concept of race does

3

not have an adequate scientific foundation. If racial designations are racist, then people ought not to be identified in the third person as members of races. And if people ought not to be identified as members of races, then individuals in the first person ought not to have racial identities.

The specific thesis of this book is that the American biracial system does not permit the identification of individuals, in the third person, as mixed race. If individuals cannot be identified, in the third person, as mixed race, then it is impossible for them to have mixed-race identities, in the first person.

To argue, in effect, that races do not exist, in the face of powerful belief structures that presuppose the existence of races and that posit racial identities for individuals, is something like tilting at windmills. So it should be made clear at the outset that this is a work of Racial Theory. Racial Theory is a new subject at this time in the twentieth century. The nineteenth century was replete with racial theories which are today recognized by well-meaning people as racist in the worst possible ways. However, there is a persistent residue of nineteenth-century racial theory, which almost everyone still accepts, and that important residue is the subject of criticism herein.

I have used traditional philosophic methods to criticize the logic of American racial designations, and less traditional but equally accessible existentialist methods to explain why Americans persist in using empirically unfounded racial designations. The cultural information about race which is herein addressed is available in Anthropology, Genetics, History, Literature, Physiology, Sociology, and commonly shared facts of American life. This means that race is an unusually discursive philosophical topic. Race is also a nontraditional philosophical topic, if only because Western philosophers have rarely addressed it directly, so far. While there is no reason for racial theory not to attract mainstream philosophic interest now, the interdisciplinary demands of the subject of race suggest that it is too deeply embedded in both ordinary and intellectual culture for philosophic interest to be proprietary.

Nevertheless, there are racial axioms in American culture

which can be conclusively addressed with the tools of analytic-empiricist philosophy. These racial axioms are logically expressed in the following schema.

> *An individual, Jay, is black if Jay has one black forebear, any number of generations back. An individual, Kay, is white if Kay has no black forebears, any number of generations back.*
> *There is no other condition for racial blackness that applies to every black individual; there is no other condition for racial whiteness that applies to every white individual.*

This schema is asymmetrical as to black and white inheritance. It logically precludes the possibility of mixed race because cases of mixed race, in which individuals have both black and white forebears, are automatically designated as cases of black race.

Historically, the schema developed along with the domination of Americans who were designated as black by Americans who were designated as white. Racial categories are primarily cultural categories: The facts of human biology and anthropology do not support a belief in the existence of racial characteristics as traits, which for any given race, are present in every individual member of that race. Nevertheless, ordinary concepts of race are based on assumptions that such support is present.

Up to this point in a philosophic analysis of race, issues of race can be addressed with the use of analytic-empiricist philosophy. And at this point it is easy to see that American racial designations are unfounded and unfair. The analysis thus far does no more than logically clarify common facts about race from science and ordinary life. Nothing new has been added to these facts, and in that sense, the analysis does not go beyond what everyone already knows. It is at this point that the question arises of why rational and otherwise well meaning Americans still make the racial designations that they do. The answer to this question has led me into existentialist-type critiques of American white racial identity, American black racial identity, and, finally, any racial identity, such that the value of mixed-race racial identity is also questionable. Scholarly existentialists may find my "commonsense existentialism" grating. I believe it is justified by the need for a language of human freedom which is strong enough to confront the shibboleths of human custom.

The necessity for a critique of customary racial designations comes from the logical breakdown of the biracial schema against the fact of the existence of individuals of mixed black and white race. All racial designations identify individuals as members of races. These identifications of individuals present the individuals with identities as members of races or else require that they construct such identities for themselves. Since mixed race does not exist in a biracial system, individuals who are of mixed race, or who would be if black and white racial categories had rational foundations, have an interesting identity problem: Either they can create identities of mixed race for themselves, in opposition to the biracial system, or, they can eschew all racial identities. This is an ambivalent position, in theory. In fact, Americans of mixed race who acknowledge at least one black forebear are rarely permitted to identify themselves in any way except as black.

The foregoing is an overview of the main ideas in this book. It is a writer's interpretation of her own work, which, as an attempt at summarization, necessarily fails, because what has required a book to say cannot be compressed into a few pages without raising new questions. The actual structure of the book unfolds less abstractly than this overview in order to accommodate the data provided by science, history, literature, and contemporary life. A chapter-by-chapter summary of that structure now follows.

Chapter 2 is an analysis of the problems with the ordinary concept of race as a natural categorization of human beings. This ordinary concept of race purports to be a concept that designates inheritable human physical characteristics, but neither the relevant scientific facts nor the uses to which the concept of race is put support this *purport*. The analytic and empirical problems with the concept of race prompt the question: Why do well-meaning and rational people still retain the concept of race? Chapter 3 answers this question with a theory of how white racism against blacks is based on white family identity. The use of existentialist philosophic tools clarifies how the ordinary behavior which supports racial designations is itself racist.

Chapter 4 is an analysis of how white family identity supports and molds ideal patterns of human breeding which result in black identification and in designated black and white races. Chapter 5 is a discussion of black family identity and a criticism of white demography. A definition of the family is suggested, which eludes not only white racial biases but all cultural biases that positivistically privilege particular forms of the family. Chapter 6 is an exploration of mixed-race family identity through mixed-race family history. At this point, the existential problems of mixed race surface in the context of identity. Note is taken of the contemporary feminist philosophical and radical political desiderata that personal identity be based on family history. However, family histories often fail to yield coherent personal identities of race for persons of mixed race. Chapters 2 through 6 constitute the remainder of Part I, *The Existential Analysis.*

The majority of designated black Americans are of mixed black and white race. The oppression of blacks by whites and the biracial American system block the possibility of personal identity based on mixed-race family history. The question therefore arises of whether there is an objective, impersonal history of mixed race in the United States on which mixed-race identity can be based. Part II, *The History of Mixed Race*, provides an answer to that question. However, the history of mixed race in the United States would merit a critical investigation in its own right because the stringency of American biracial designation raises questions of how mixed-race individuals have been dealt with and of what sort of existence they have had in the past. The legal, sociological, intellectual, ideological, and literary aspects of the history of mixed race are explored in relation to the biracial American system in Chapters 7 through 12. Chapter 13 concludes Part II with notes on the special racial alienation of Americans of mixed race.

The alienation of Americans of mixed race from even normal forms of alienation raises new questions of mixed racial identity: Would an American identity of mixed race be desirable? Is such an identity worth creating? The question of the good faith or bad faith inherent in such a possible identity is addressed in Chapter 14; Sartre's critical description of the French anti-Semite is used as a test for a possible identity of American mixed race. Overall, this exercise in Chapter 14 does not support the positive value of such an identity. However, although Part III is titled *The Philosophy of Anti-Race*, a strong argument against all racial identities is not formulated, partly out of respect for the overwhelming attachment that Americans have to their black and white racial identifications and identities, and partly because I think it is necessary to allow time for discussion of such an issue to develop. Chapter 15 is a linguistic analysis of American racial words, which is meant to emphasize their metaphorical nature. There is a somewhat superficial suggestion that "gray" be introduced into the vocabulary as a designation for mixed black and white race. However, the oppressiveness of some racial designations and the *immanence* of all of them, combined with the lack of an empirical foundation for the concept of race, entail that no racial words are appropriate designations for human beings.

2

The Ordinary Concept of Race

Race is a primary concept in American culture. Once a person is racially designated black or white, the designation does not normally require further qualification. Many important opportunities and boundaries in ordinary life depend on racial designations. Therefore the criteria for the initial and final racial designation of an individual ought to be clear and fair.

It is ordinarily assumed that when an individual is designated black or white, the individual has some physical characteristics and does not have some other physical characteristics—the ordinary concept of race purports to refer to an individual's body. However, the ordinary concept of race rests solely on a kinship schema of racial inheritance: If a person has a black parent, a black grandparent, or a black great^n-grandparent (where n is the number of generations in the past and can be any degree of ancestry), then that person is considered black. But if a person has a white parent, or three white grandparents, or Z white great^n-grandparents (where Z is any odd number and n is still any degree of ancestry), then that person is not thereby considered white. This schema unjustly excludes people with black forebears from white designation.[1] More precisely, the injustice of the kinship schema can be presented this way, if we suppose that *Alpha* could be anyone:

(1) If Alpha has a black ancestor, Alpha is black.
(2) If Alpha is black, Alpha is treated unjustly.
(3) If Alpha has a black ancestor, Alpha is treated unjustly.
(4) Therefore, it is unjust to say that Alpha is black if Alpha has a black ancestor.

9

It could be objected that while (3) is obviously entailed in (1) and (2), the conclusion, (4), does not follow from (1) and (2): It is a fact of life that people are black if they have black ancestors, and, like many facts of life, it may be unfair that some people are black and therefore subject to injustice; but the fact of their blackness and the ancestral basis of their blackness is not itself an injustice. This objection would hold if the kinship system had an empirical foundation, i.e., if it were a fact that (1) If Alpha has a black ancestor, Alpha is black. It is not a fact that Alpha is black if Alpha has a black ancestor, because there is nothing in the world to which the term 'black' refers in the bodies of all individuals to whom that term is applied. It should become clear in this chapter that the kinship system does not rest on any scientific facts about race, because there are no scientific facts about race that support the ordinary concept of race. There are historical facts about 'race' as a social concept. During the historical origins of the modern, ordinary concept of race, scientific beliefs that have since been disproved were used to justify the historical origins of racial oppression. But this does not imply that either history or science provides an empirical foundation for that ordinary concept of race, which purports to refer to the physical characteristics of individuals. At this point, before examining those facts of history and science that appear to provide a foundation for the ordinary concept of race, it might be helpful to return to the ordinary criteria for racial designation that are expressed in the model of the asymmetrical kinship system.

The Kinship Schema of Black and White
Racial Inheritance

There is a strong asymmetry between black and white racial inheritance. If a person has a black parent, a black grandparent, or a black $great^n$-grandparent (where n represents any number of past generations), then that person is designated black. But if a person has a white parent, or three white grandparents, or Z white $great^n$-grandparents (where Z is any odd number and n still represents any number of past generations), then that person is not thereby designated white. A fortiori, anyone with white forebears equal in number to the black forebears who would result in their being designated black is not thereby designated white. Thus whiteness is the absence of black forebears, assuming no other *non-white* forebears, or the absence of non-white forebears. And blackness is the presence of one or more black forebears, depending on how far back it is considered necessary or desirable to go in investigating the race of a person's forebears. This means that in order to be white it is necessary that an individual be all white, while in order to be black it is sufficient if an individual has one black forebear.[2]

The logic of this schema allows that the sufficient condition of one black forebear need never be satisfied in any way that can be empirically verified. Black designation is based on an individual's location anywhere in a line of descent that contains one black forebear. A black forebear is thereby defined as someone who is in a line of descent where there is one black forebear. Logically this is an infinite regress.

The schema implies that both whiteness and blackness are defined in terms of blackness. Thus American racial categories are interdependent, and because there is no positive definition of blackness, American racial categories are groundless—they have no empirical foundation.

But although the kinship schema, as a model, expresses the logical structure of the American system of black and white racial designation, it does not completely capture the ordinary concept of race. Ordinarily, when an individual is designated white or black by self or others, something more than the race(s) of forebears seems to be at issue. It seems to be the case that racial designations refer to those physical characteristics of individuals which are not only inherited from their forebears but that inhere in individuals in some physical way. Thus if someone is 'black,' in common American usage, this seems to be a fact about that individual's physical body *and about the bodies of all other individuals so designated.*[3] In order to evaluate these physical implications of the ordinary concept of race, it is necessary to understand the historical and scientific background of the ordinary concept of race. There is, to be sure, some restricted scientific foundation for the ordinary concept of race, which is based on accepted empirical laws of heredity. However, it is not this restricted scientific foundation that people have in mind when they use the ordinary concept of race. What they have in mind are older, disproved scientific theories of race, which have now passed into the realm of mythology, according to twentieth-century scientists. What scientists now view as the mythology of race is closely intertwined with the historical conditions under which the now-disproved scientific theories of race were formulated.

The History and Biology of the Concept of Race

Many historians trace references to racial differences back to antiquity. Less formally, some religious fundamentalists read racial differentiations in the biblical account of Noah's descendants.[4] However, there appears to be a contemporary consensus that the modern concept of race, which underlies the concept of race formed in the United States during the period of black slavery, has its roots in the European seventeenth-, eighteenth-, and nineteenth-century colonial expansions into what is now called the Third World.[5] The dominated and exploited non-European populations of this (present) Third World were conceptualized by Europeans as racial populations. It has been suggested that this racial conceptualization was developed by European invaders as a justification or rationalization of their domination of Third World peoples and of the subsequent European and American exploitation of the labor and natural resources of these peoples.[6] As the racial designations of the Third World populations were developed, these peoples were judged by Europeans to be less advanced culturally than Europeans. The allegedly less advanced non-European cultures were held to be inferior to European cultures—to the extent that Europeans acknowledged that Third World peoples even had cultures. In European thinking, this judged cultural inferiority of non-European peoples was linked to their non-white racial designations.[7]

It was generally believed during the colonial period that the racial designations of Third World peoples referred to biological

THE EXISTENTIAL ANALYSIS

characteristics, which were inherited within the races in question. The widespread model of racial inheritance was some kind of arithmetic mechanism which dictated the intergenerational transmission of racial characteristics through their division in the blood of offspring.[8] For example, in the United States, during the nineteenth century, it was believed that an individual with one black parent and one white parent was one-half white and one-half black. If that individual had a child with a white person, then the child would be one-quarter black. It was believed that a black individual was all black and that his or her descendants inherited their race in simple, divisible units, which, through the dilution of blood, became fractions of the resulting offspring. People whose blood had not thereby been mixed or diluted (before their birth) were racially pure. It is not difficult to see the relation between this theory of the dilution of the blood through racial mixing and the kinship schema of racial inheritance. It may be that as a model of racial designation, the kinship schema is the logical structure of practical applications of the blood theory.

By about 1900, biologists and anthropologists began to realize that there were serious empirical problems with both the fractional concept of racial inheritance and the idea of pure races. The problem with the fractional concept of racial inheritance is that the physical characteristics which can be used for racial designation are caused by genes that vary independently of one another during the process of human conception. In lay terms, these are the genetic facts that are now commonly accepted by scientists: Each individual receives a full complement of genes in two halves, one-half from each parent; each parent contributes one-half of his or her total of genetic material to the offspring. These genetic facts do not support the belief that there is, ever has been, or ever will be a pure race. All human beings are members of the same species, and all of the inheritable physical differences among them are the result of their varied genetic makeup. It is not that racial characteristics are subject to dilution but that the genes that underlie racial characteristics are subject to dispersal into different combinations. Each gene responsible for a racial—or any other—characteristic retains its complete identity as long as it remains in the gene pool, i.e., as long as it is capable of being copied for combination with other genes at the time of conception. Even apart from this integrity of individual genes through inheritance, it does not make sense to think of 'old' or 'inherited' biological material persisting in descendants. Genes function by providing instructions for the development of new biological material—old biological material does not persist over generations in any form that can be diluted or mixed.

All human beings belong to the same species. All designated human races are capable of interbreeding. In scientific terms, a race is merely a self-contained breeding population that has a higher percentage of individuals with certain designated physical characteristics than some other population. *The scientific racial unit is the breeding population as a whole and not any individual within the population.* All individuals within a race do not have the same racial characteristics. The racial differences between any two individuals within a race may be greater than the racial differences (or physical differences designated as racial) between some individuals within that race and some individuals within another race. For example, there may be greater varieties in body structure among American blacks than between some blacks and some whites; some blacks have lighter skin than some whites; some whites have woolier hair than some blacks. Such variations in racial characteristics result from the fact that the genes which cause racial characteristics do not all get inherited together. Not all blacks have all of the genes that result in black racial designations. In logical, causal terms, there are no necessary, necessary and sufficient, or sufficient racial characteristics, or genes for such characteristics, which every member of a race has.[9]

As for the old idea of blood, there is nothing in the divisions of the major human blood groups which corresponds to the divisions of the major human racial groups. The four major human blood groups, which are identifiable in terms of their compatibility for transfusion purposes, are distributed somewhat geographically over the globe, but there is no connection between the racial characteristics of an individual's parents and that individual's blood group. Not only does blood not mix and not become diluted through interracial heredity but it is possible that close relatives of the same racial designation may have incompatible blood types for transfusion purposes.[10]

Ever since the 1920s, after Franz Boas corrected his earlier claims that cultural behavior was physically inheritable, social scientists have been careful to disassociate the behavioral or cultural characteristics of racially designated groups from the inheritance of physical racial characteristics. They have made this separation because there is no empirical evidence for such hereditary connections.[11] Many biologists and anthropologists are skeptical of the concept of race as a useful scientific tool because no racial population, past or present, has ever been completely isolated from other races in terms of breeding. Furthermore, there are too many variables in genetic combinations, including mutation, for individuals to breed 'true to type' over long periods of time. The scientific consensus that there are three main human racial groups is grudging, at best.[12]

Despite the scientific problems with biological concepts of race, social scientists have been reluctant to suggest that races do not exist in the sense in which the ordinary person believes that they exist. The reason for this reluctance seems to be not only that the ordinary belief in races is widespread but that this widespread belief is connected with strong feelings.[13] This reluctance should not be surprising, because while it may be part of the job of social scientists to analyze concepts which underlie human behavior, social scientists are not obligated to criticize such concepts. The criticism of a concept, such as the concept of physical race, is a task for philosophers (and perhaps other social critics).

The main philosophic criticism of the ordinary concept of physical race is this: There are no clear and uniform criteria by which the ordinary concept of race can be applied to every individual. And because racial designations have important consequences in the lives of individuals so designated, this lack of clarity and uniformity means that racial designations based on the ordinary concept of race are not fair.

It could be objected that there is nothing wrong with the ordinary concept of race, just as there is nothing wrong with the ordinary concepts of chair, cat, or tree. Many concepts are applied in varying ways based on different criteria of application, which may not even be predictable, independently of contexts, from application to application. This is not a problem with the concepts in question but merely a fact about the complexity of human meanings and cultural-linguistic behavior. Thus (the objection would continue) there are no necessary and sufficient conditions that all objects which can be counted as chairs must have. And there may be no *essences* possessed in common by all cats or all trees. Some individuals can be seen to be *paradigm* instances of racial whiteness and racial blackness, and their forebears had the same (respective) appearances as the observed individuals. Therefore the existence of a *slippery slope* in the form of individuals of mixed race does not mean that the primary concepts of pure race are illusory.

The answer to this objection needs to be as far-reaching as the objection itself, because the objection gestures toward the totality of those very habits of cultural life which the foregoing philosophical criticism of the ordinary concept of physical race attempts to challenge. First, it doesn't matter how concepts of things such as chairs are expanded and reinvented; but this expansion and reinvention are very important with concepts of people, which determine how those people will be treated. Second, concepts of cats and trees remain valid or appropriate without a cat or tree essence, because there are necessary and sufficient conditions that beings must fulfill in order to be counted as cats or trees. Lions, for example, are a natural kind that can be conceptualized without recourse to a lion essence, because they fulfill not only the necessary and sufficient conditions for membership in the group of cats but the necessary and sufficient conditions for membership in the subgroup of great cats and the sub-subgroup of lions. In contrast, those human groups that are designated as racial groups do not constitute a species or subgroup within the larger natural group of *Homo sapiens*. Races may be analogous to those subgroups known as 'breeds' among domestic animals. But while everyone acknowledges that collies and holsteins, for example, are the result of human control over animal reproduction, or human animal-breeding, it is less commonly acknowledged that paradigm ideals of pure American blacks and pure American whites are the result of human control over human reproduction, i.e., the result of human-human breeding.

Thus there are no racial essences which give meaning to the concept of race, there are no necessary and sufficient conditions for racial membership, and races are not natural kinds. Finally, the existence of individuals who appear to be racially pure does not rescue the concept of race, because this concept requires that the majority of humans be and always have been racially pure. And racial purity is not a general truth about the human condition. Thus the slippery slope of mixed race is more than an unusual exception to a statistical norm or paradigm of racial purity. But even if instances of mixed race were statistical exceptions, these exceptions would be not a merely theoretical objection to concepts of racial purity but facts of human existence. Such facts of human existence, of the existence of human beings who belie commonsense racial concepts, ought to be an overriding axiological consideration. That is, if the existence of certain human beings causes problems for certain concepts or systems of categorization, then it is the concepts or systems of categorization and not the human existants which need to be criticized and changed.

The black emancipatory tradition in the United States has recognized the weakness of the concept of physical race for a long time, at least since W.E.B. Du Bois.[14] Du Bois was aware of the lack of an empirical foundation in nature for the concept of race. In the following literary exchange between himself as the narrator and a white man who would be considered a racist today, Du Bois suggests that the concept of the black race is the result of white injustice against blacks:

> "But what is this group; and how do you differentiate it; and how do you call it 'black' when you admit it is not black?"
> I recognize it quite easily and with full legal sanction; the black man is a person who must ride "Jim Crow" in Georgia.[15]

However, Du Bois and other important writers in the black emancipatory tradition resist racism on the basis of their own acceptance of the concept of race. This kind of resistance to the injustices that are perpetrated by whites against blacks obligates blacks to argue that their educational, moral, social, legal, and economic deficits in comparison to whites are not physically inherited or necessarily acquired.[16] But there is no sustained objection to ordinary racial designations within the tradition of black emancipation.

The ordinary concept of race in the United States has no scientific foundation. Yet rational people still retain this concept. The question is, why? What purpose does the ordinary concept of race serve? What prevents otherwise rational people from abandoning this concept as a means of designating individuals? To answer these questions, one must look at how racial designation determines ordinary identity in ordinary existence.

3

White Family Identity

The scientific concept of physical race does not support the ordinary concept of race in the United States. This ordinary concept of race rests on an asymmetrical kinship system, which has the logic of an infinite regress: A person is black if she has a black forebear, and that forebear was black if she had a black forebear, and so on. This *one-drop rule*, which has been in effect since about 1915, is in theory more stringent than the Third Reich's designation of Jews. The Nazis designated a person as a Jew if that person had one grandparent who observed the Jewish religion.[1]

The infinite regress that is built into the asymmetrical kinship system is a theoretical problem. In American reality, the ordinary concept of race has a power in people's lives that no merely logical argument can dispel. Although the American one-drop rule is unusual in its stringency, the broad concept of race in contemporary usage does resonate with concepts of family and heredity, which are part of a wide European tradition. The English word "race" has its source in the French word *race* or *rase*, which was adapted from the Italian word *razzo*; the Italian word in turn was adapted from the Spanish word *raza*. In this background, 'race' meant a group of people with a common ancestor, or a *line* of descent, where the term 'line' was expressed by the same word as the word for a written line. In view of this background, it is not surprising that the concept 'race' should be connected with ideas of kinship.[2] However, in the European background, an individual's race would have been that individual's particular family. In contrast, in the modern American meaning of the term 'race,' an individual's particular family is viewed as a medium for assigning that individual to an abstract category of race. That is, when an individual is racially designated according to the kinship schema, the individual is not identified as a member of a particular biological family, as a final identification, but identified as an instantiation of a general racial category, because that individual's kin can be racially designated.

The Western cultural belief that human traits which determine social status are hereditary was probably the result of a similar process of abstraction. Thus at one time individual leaders may have been believed to pass their noble traits on to their descendants. At some point a general concept of noble or desirable traits was formed, and students of human nature assumed that anyone exhibiting such traits had to have noble ancestors. Eventually, this assumption found expression in quasi-scientific programs to trace the genealogy of "superior" individuals. The idea was that such programs would eventually lend empirical support to *Eugenics*, or controlled and directed human breeding with the goal of "producing superior" individuals.[3] In general, neither the attempts to provide an empirical basis for Eugenics nor eugenic practices have been effective or successful. Nevertheless, the persistence of theories about the inheritability of intelligence or intelligence quotients (IQs) shows that the eugenic quest dies hard.[4] And the abstract concept of race, although officially shorn of any behavioral connotations in liberal thinking, still functions as a powerful medium for residual ideas of hereditary human traits. Individuals are assigned to races as physical designations, and the cultures of the races they are assigned to are still used to explain their behavior.

Not only are racial modes of thought used by well-meaning people to explain how other people behave in their own cultures, but scholars assume that the same modes of thought dominate other cultures. For example, when M. I. Finley writes about the ideologies accompanying slavery in the ancient world, he speaks of race despite an "absence of skin-colour stigma." As Finley puts it, "The issue is not of a concept of 'race' acceptable to modern biologists or of a properly defined and consistently held concept,

THE EXISTENTIAL ANALYSIS

but of the view commonly taken in ordinary disc⟨
now" (italics mine).[5]

Indeed, this ordinary view of race, which Finley n.
ing into ancient sources with his "then as now," is not
interpretations of the Western tradition. It has been p⟨
scholars of Indian history, of Chinese history, and of peo⟨ ⌐s and
cultures in virtually all times and places.[6]

I have suggested that the ordinary concept of physical race in
the United States should be analyzed philosophically. The *work-in-
life* performed by this ordinary concept of race needs to be understood—the concept of physical race requires an existential meaning, or, more precisely, the workings of the ordinary concept of
race in ordinary life should be conceptualized. Such a conceptualization would be in the tradition of an existential analysis. Within
an existential analysis, a point of view is usually important. It is
from the point of view of white people in the United States that the
existential analysis of the work-in-life of the ordinary concept of
physical race ought to proceed. This is because the dominant racial
group in the United States is the group that is designated white,
and white Americans actively carry on the dominant cultural tradition within which the modern concept of race was developed.

During the modern colonial period, the ordinary concept of
physical race was applied to non-European people, at the same
time that modern forms of domination and exploitation were imposed on these designated non-white people. This historical background of the modern concept of physical race should be part of
the context of an existential analysis of that concept. But the origin
of a concept is not the same thing as the present existential work
done by that concept. The origin could be malign and the work-in-
life benign. However, not only was the origin of the ordinary
American concept of physical race racist but the current work-in-
life of the concept is racist as well.

The concept of the black or Negro race in the United States
originated in the institution of black or Negro slavery in this country.[7] In general, the closer one gets to the discourse of American
slave owners, the stronger are the posited differences between the
black and white races, to the devaluation of the black race.[8] But

the (existential) work-in-life of the concept of race no longer has to do with slavery, except perhaps as a historical context, which has value-positive, value-negative, and value-neutral moments in the rhetoric of varied discourses. Existentially, the concept of race now works in the lives of white Americans, who have white pasts, white futures, and white present projects. From a white point of view, the concept of race has to do with white families—more precisely, with how the white family is conceptualized. A philosophic understanding of how the ordinary concept of physical race works in thought about white families would not necessarily imply anything about how black families are conceptualized. In fact, the way that the concept of physical race works in conceptualizing white families has made it impossible for many designated black people to use the concept of family to conceptualize black families. This is usually interpreted as a cultural tragedy but, in terms of individual freedom, it may be an asset, because it makes it necessary to "liberate" the concept of the family, as I indicate later.[9]

If white people did not use the ordinary concept of physical race, black people would have no need to claim the concept of physical race from their own point of view, as a basis on which to create "positive identities." Indeed, quite often in individual life stories it is the childhood realization of the social fact that one is a designated black person which is the most hurtful racial fact psychologically. And this damage may or may not rest on previously imbibed white racist beliefs. If white racist beliefs about blacks have been accepted before the designation is made, the early realized designation has the power to shame and frighten individuals, who then see themselves identified with the least attractive, most underprivileged, and most harshly punished designated black individuals, namely, those who fill the positions of stereotypes.[10] A resistance against the identification with the stereotypes, with what W.E.B. Du Bois called "the worst" of the Negro race, has often had the strength to propel lifelong projects to "prove" that the identification is an error. The proof can be directed toward falsifying the stereotype, toward establishing an individual exception to the stereotype, or away from any black identification. If the goal

THE EXISTENTIAL ANALYSIS

of these projects is to dispel racism, they are probably all doomed to failure, because racism is not a theoretical stance that can be proved or disproved.[11] The point here is not to lament reactivity or to criticize waste of human energy but to make it clear that the American concept of physical race originates in the existential points of view of people who are designated white. *I will discuss.*

If white racist beliefs about blacks are unknown to individuals before they are racially designated, then the designation itself stamps an important *otherness* on the individual in question, who is usually a child. Aside from separate treatment, which may or may not be equal, to know that one is 'other' cannot but obligate one to construct a special 'other' self-identity. If there are no sound grounds for this identification as 'other,' the identity which rests on such an identification would have to be a "false" or *inau-thentic* identity. *b Part of the human condition.*

In the United States, racial emancipatory discourse is a historical tradition, which began with protests against slavery. After slavery had been abolished, the discourse moved to arguments against the inheritability or inevitable acquisition of the socially undesirable traits and behavior of people designated black. It could be said that first enslavement and then undesirable traits and behavior were removed from the concept of the black race. What is left is an ordinary concept of a physical black race, which, although unsupported by science, is still strong enough to support many of the forms of racism against blacks that are thought and practiced by both designated black people and designated white people. This is the concept of physical race which is analyzed existentially herein, although there are a few more caveats and qualifications to get out of the way first.

There is a distinction between two forms of white racism against blacks. The implication is not that racism occurs only neatly divided into those two forms or that there are not multiple types within each form.[12] Rather, the distinction between these two forms blocks references to goodwill or good intentions as bases for objections to a general claim that the concept of physical race is racist in the malign meaning of the term 'racist.'[13] The necessary distinction is between *intentional racism* and *unintentional racism*.

Unintentional racism involves assumptions that blacks (and perhaps other people of color as well) are not included in the important activities of one's life. It is not necessary always to be aware of one's own whiteness while living in this exclusion; one simply lives in a white world and non-whites are only occasional and unimportant agents in that world. For example, one does not invite black people to one's party because one does not know any black people who could be invited; one does not hire a black person for the job because there are no black candidates. By contrast, intentional racism entails a frequent or constant awareness that one is white, accompanied by strong value-negative judgments against blacks. For example, one avoids social situations in which black people are present for the sole reason that black people are present; one does not hire the black candidate for the job simply because the candidate is black. This intentional racism may require that some value-positive, white physical standard, such as "blood in the face" or the ability to blush visibly, be met before a person is designated white.[14] An intentional racist is likely to be self-conscious about being a racist and to hold speculations about racial purity, racial religious genealogy, and racially inherited traits and behavior, speculations which stand out as ideological.[15]

An unintentional white racist need only vaguely believe in the existence of physical races and treat people differently on the basis of their perceived or designated race, to the extent that broad cultural norms prescribe or permit such treatment. As the cultural norms become less biased against designated black people, unintentional racists usually adjust to the changes, with varying degrees of verbal and social resistance. However, intentional racists, from Reconstruction-era Ku Klux Klanners to contemporary Aryan Skinheads, offer active resistance to egalitarian social changes that benefit designated black people; this resistance takes the form of strong verbal denunciation and abuse, illegal acts of violence, and perhaps efforts to work through official forms of political organization.[16]

The large group of unintentional white racists are the mass of reasonable, goodwilled, law-abiding white citizens, as they present themselves publicly. They do not present themselves as racists be-

THE EXISTENTIAL ANALYSIS

cause that term is usually reserved for intentional racists. The un-intentional racists accept the legal rights of blacks, respect the aspirations of black Americans who wish to "better" themselves in the American way, and may support affirmative action programs in employment and education. But it is not farfetched to call these people "racist," as a collectivity, because they are the American majority upholding the traditions that result in the oppression of black people in this society.[17] The key question, then, is this: How does racism perpetuate itself in the midst of legal rights for blacks, employment and educational opportunities for blacks, and public goodwill toward the aspirations of blacks by the reasonable white majority?

It has been suggested that the concept of physical race itself supports racism. This chapter began with the claim that logical points and scientific facts are not sufficient to do away with the ordinary concept of physical race, because the concept does important work-in-life for white people. What exactly is this existential work done by the ordinary concept of physical race?

The ordinary concept of physical race does the existential work of perpetuating the concept of the white family for unintentional, as well as intentional, white racists. This concept of the white family is defined by the asymmetrical kinship schema of racial inheritance. An individual, A, is white if A has no black forebears. This means that A is white if A's genealogical family consisting of forebears in direct lines of descent are, each of them, white. The only way that A can ensure that the family of A's creation is white is if the co-parents of all of A's children are genealogically white in the same way in which A is genealogically white. A's children, grandchildren, and great^n-grandchildren will have to meet the same requirements if A's family in the future is to remain white. What is more, if A's entire family is to include uncles, aunts, cousins, and the like, each of them will also have to meet the same kinship requirements if A's entire family is to be considered white. That is, individuals are white if their families are white, in both a genealogical and an extended sense of family, and a family is white if and only if each family member is white.

In meeting these requirements of family whiteness, it does not matter whether or not A believes that physical racial characteristics are accompanied by desirable or undesirable traits and behavior, because regardless of whether or not physical racial characteristics are so accompanied, one designated black family member is sufficient to negate the whiteness of the entire genealogical family, which consists of a line of descent, and of the extended family that includes aunts, uncles, cousins, and the like.

Anthony Appiah, writing about *racisms*, provides a useful distinction between extrinsic racism and intrinsic racism. The extrinsic racist believes that as a (contingent) matter of fact, people of different races have different moral value. The intrinsic racist believes that racial differences alone have moral value.[18] Concerning family relations, the ordinary white person, who may be an unintentional racist, is required to be an intrinsic racist. The inclusion in a white family of a person B, with a black forebear, is not merely a matter concerning the relation between some members of the family and B, because B's inclusion in the family can have an automatic effect on how all other members of the family are racially designated, as well as on the racial designation of the family as a collectivity. Thus not only does kinship determine race but *race determines the race of kin.*

Once one fully understands this *genetic logic* of white family relations, one can begin to understand why ordinary Americans continue to believe in a concept of physical race that is not supported by modern science and which is unjust to people who have both black and white forebears. A good part of the identities of many Americans is determined by the identities of their families, which include living relations as well as the dead and yet to be born. Almost all designated white individuals belong to designated white families, and there is no way in which a racially white family can avoid being intrinsically racist concerning its membership if it is to retain its white racial identity.

Physical characteristics that are designated as racial in individuals are by definition inheritable. These characteristics vary widely within the group of designated black people, and there is no one set of such characteristics that gets passed on as a set during all events of conception. But each physical racial characteristic exists in an individual only if that individual has inherited it—this is true by definition. And each physical racial characteristic can be passed on during some event of conception, although it cannot be predicted which or even if any physical characteristic will be passed on during any one event of conception.

Designated black physical racial characteristics are genetic. The mechanism of human genetics is heterosexual sexual intercourse. That fact alone is enough to account for much of the obscenity, fear, fascination, lust, scorn, degradation, and both real and pseudo-revulsion with which white people have considered the sexuality of black people. Individuals who are designated black have the ability, through the mechanism of their heterosexuality, to destroy the white identity of white families and, because race of kin determines race of individuals, to destroy the white identity of the relatives of their descendants. Thus the asymmetrical kinship system of racial inheritance in the United States not only is intrinsically racist in favor of white people, but it defines black people as intrinsically threatening and dangerous to white families.

As uncomfortable, painful, and dangerous as it has always been to be a designated black person in the United States, the concerns, restrictions, insecurity, and fundamental negations in having a designated white identity are not trivial. This white identity, based on white family membership, probably comes as close as any existential situation can to instantiating Martin Heidegger's analysis of human ontology in *Being and Time*.[19] In this context, it is ironic that Heidegger publicly supported the Nazis for ten months and that he may have had his own private, lifelong program of "National Socialism."[20] I have to compound that irony (in Richard Rorty's sense) by making free with some of Heidegger's "passing theories" (again in Richard Rorty's sense, of his reading of Donald Davidson) to discuss white American racism in what follows.[21]

A designated white person's necessary belief in the concept of physical race gives that person's past, present, and future a unity based on an absence, a nothingness in that person's racial identity.

The white person, A, who occupies a privileged place in American society does so on the basis of assumptions that can never be proved because they are universal negative statements, namely:

None of A's forebears is non-white;
None of A's descendants is non-white;
None of A's lateral relations is non-white.

All three of these universal negations must be true for A to have a white identity based on membership in a family which has a white identity. Furthermore, for A to be white, the three assumptions must be true of every member of A's family. And to be non-white or, in this case, black means nothing more than that A have at least one non-white or black family member. Therefore the sole determinant of A's whiteness is the absence of any individual who is defined by the presence of one individual who cannot be defined by the absence of those individuals whose absence defines A. And not even something like a cherished stigmata of "blood in the face" can save A from this foundation of negations, because those who do not have the absences necessary to enjoy the same privileges that A enjoys may also have "blood in the face"—that is, there are designated black people in the United States who are able to blush visibly.[22]

Indeed, any positive characteristic which is added to A's white identity that is based on family identity will be a fact about individuals or their behavior which could also be true of racially designated blacks. There are some positive attributes of white families that are not likely to be shared by black families. For example, members of the white family to which A belongs may have occupied high political office in the past, and this may be less likely to be true of a black person. But the causes of the differences between white and black families—causes that point to the self-perpetuating character of white breeding (about which more is said later)—need to be understood in the historical context of the disadvantaged position of designated black people in the United States. Such historical contexts are contingent and no one knows that the future will resemble the past. (Not only the normal problems with induction concerning knowledge of the future but forces of historical contingency itself are at work here, so that the long view of history provides no security for believing that certain nation states will always endure or that certain designated races will always have the cultural privilege that they have had so far.)[23] However, historical facts about racially designated groups, individuals, and families are part of their ethnicity, and ethnicity is not the same thing as physically designated race. The ordinary concept of physical race is not normally applied as a reference to history.

At the time Heidegger was reinstated in German academic life, after exile for Nazi collaboration, he experienced the legendary turning, or *kehre*, in his thought. After this *kehre* when Heidegger addressed the confrontation between modern man and technology, he might have been talking about the separation between physical race and ethnicity. Technology has made a strong contribution to that separation in the form of studies of differences in cultures by social scientists and research about human genetics by biologists. Technology has also made all human groups mobile geographically, and this loss of homelands, which is another post-*kehre* theme of Heidegger's, also creates changes in ethnicity.[24]

The modern separation of race from ethnicity creates, on the part of (white) *Dasein*, ethnisms which tend to glorify older ideas of race. Thus Heidegger himself believed that his French disciples had to learn how to think in the German language in order to be able to think at all. Heidegger also believed that the solutions to the problems posed by technology could be found only through studies of pre-Socratic Greek thought, studies that had to be conducted through German thinkers such as the poet Frederick Hölderlin. And in the famous *Der Spiegel* interview that Heidegger authorized in 1966 for posthumous publication, he made it quite clear that the great work of interrogating the essence of technology could be done only by noncosmopolitan Germans, Germans who knew the Black Forest meaning of the term 'wood-path' (as he himself did).[25] Furthermore, it should be noted that according to Heidegger, science is secondary to technology: Technology is more fundamental and *leading* than science.[26] This is important, because many non-Western cultures have had highly developed sciences, but no culture in the known history of humanity has come close to the technological developments that have been concomitant with the dominance of designated white Westerners in modern history.

Physical racial identity must now do some of the work previously done by concepts combining physical and ethnic racial identity. Therefore, those who need to hold onto the concept of their white racial identity in times of increasing cultural progress for blacks—and all whites who value their white family identities have this need—will become more intrinsically racist. Indeed, many observers think that this is exactly what is happening on the "wood-path," or "grass-roots," level of American culture.[27] To return to Appiah's terms, as extrinsic racism loses ground, intrinsic racism increases in intensity. This happens due to the importance of family identity for whites and the combined forces of modern science, modern technology, and modern social policy, which leave white family identity with nothing to rest on except intrinsic racial identity. The possibility of genetically engineering physical racial characteristics, a technological possibility Heidegger was aware of in principle, suggests that even the negative foundation of white family identity that is provided by white racial identity may also be lost.[28]

Before going further with this analysis, it might be helpful to review the previous steps. There is no scientific basis for the ordinary concept of race, and ordinary racial designations are based on an asymmetrical kinship schema of racial inheritance. The scientific facts and the logical inadequacies of the kinship schema are not enough to abolish the ordinary concept of race and it is reasonable to ask why. Why do white people still hold onto this ordinary concept of physical race? The answer is that the ordinary concept of physical race is a matter not merely of individual identity and privilege but of identity and privilege *for-the-sake-of* white family identity and privilege. People are white if they belong to white families, and their white families can remain white only if designated black people have been, are, and will be excluded from them. This exclusion for-the-sake-of the family is an intrinsic racist exclusion—the only criterion for exclusion is designated black race, because of the possibility of inheritable designated black racial characteristics. In other words, many unintentionally racist white people who might support the aspirations of designated black people and egalitarian social change are intentional racists when it comes to their families.

To return to the Heideggerian analysis, white family identity instantiates ontological structures of *concern* and *being-with*. White *Dasein* is *thrown-into-the-world* as a member of a white family for which it is *concerned* and about whose members it *cares*. Caring is particular, when *authentic*. White *Dasein cares* about its own particular children, on the basis of its realization of its *not-being* (non-white), which comes from the *not* (non-whiteness) of its white family.[29] That is, white Americans know that if their children and their children's children are racially designated black, their lives will be uncomfortable, painful, and endangered. So before those children are conceived, white *Daseins resolve* that these children will have no non-white forebears. This resolve is not a merely formal matter (for example, Hans Jonas suggests that Heidegger's decision to join the National Socialists might have been the result of merely formal *resolve*) but a resoluteness based on the contingencies of white *Dasein's factical* conditions in *being-thrown-into-the-world* as white *Dasein*.[30] = non-black race

The exclusionary nature of white resolve for-the-sake-of white children is a serious matter. A contemporary intentional white racist poster depicts a white man and a white woman bending over a white infant. The top of the poster has the text, "It is a simple reality that," and the bottom reads, "To be born WHITE is an honor and a privilege [*sic*]."[31] But even W.E.B. Du Bois excused black Americans for choosing mates with light skin on the grounds that it is natural and proper to want to give one's children whatever social advantages one can. Does this not suggest that designated black Americans ought to be able to *understand* the exclusionary resoluteness of the white family? And does this understanding entail *support*, a *standing-under* the exclusionary resoluteness? Ought those who are excluded from white families to accept their exclusion and submit to the privilege and dominance of white families, quietly, out of concern for the children or at least out of *respect*, as in looking at the situation again?[32]

There are no easy answers to these questions. The logic of the situation requires that anyone who is serious about doing away with intrinsic racism cannot support the concept of the white family in the United States. This is not to say that the concept of family cannot be supported. It is to say that the structures of family identity must be seriously examined, from *all* racial points of view.

4

Black Family Identity

The intentional and intrinsically racist asymmetrical kinship schema of white racial identification is the locus of white family identity in the United States. This schema of white family identification is not a natural schema of human reproduction; it is very easy for humans to reproduce in ways that are out of phase with the schema. It takes a resolve for the sake of the white family to reproduce in ways which are in phase with the schema. However, the schema is not a positive or prescriptive genetic model, because no specific genes or even genetic characteristics are identified by the schema; rather, individuals who may or may not have proscribed genes or genetic characteristics are excluded from participating in the schema because of their kinship to other individuals who are presumed to have proscribed genes and genetic characteristics. From a white point of view, the schema is not a model of human inheritance but a prescription for human breeding.

The schema is a prescription for breeding designated white individuals and white families. Traditionally, designated white families have had greater political, economic, and social advantages than families of any other racial designation in the United States.[1] These American white families are a nineteenth- and twentieth-century expression of a tradition that privileges the family as a private institution in Western nations.[2]

33

The Modern Position of the White Family

The development of modern Western technology is a danger to the traditional ethnicity of the white family, because this technology has severed the connection between white ethnicity and white physical race, in principle if not always in fact. But the dominance of the white family in the modern West has developed along with the dominance of modern Western technology, and it would not be an exaggeration to call the American white family the standard-bearer or avant-garde of this technology. The American white family can hold its own against the incursions of technology on traditional associations of ethnicity with physical race, but this can be done only if the family becomes more intrinsically and intentionally racist about its physical white racial identity (and, as a result, perhaps more racist in nonfamily matters as well). Technology can compensate the white family for the loss of its white cultural ethnicity by providing the white family with ever-evolving novelties in place of its older ethnicity. These technological novelties structure every phase of white family life, including health, education, life-styles, military and civil service, child care, reproduction, beauty, work, recreation, and so on, depending on how the various activities of the modern family are catalogued.

The white American family may or may not be able to survive the depredations of modern technology on the natural environment. But, in general, it is probably better able to survive these depredations than any other racially designated family type, because as the predominant family type within the Western ruling classes, it skims off the best necessities, comforts, and luxuries of modern technology for itself.

Miscegenation as a Historical Problem

The official American white family, which is a publicly sanctioned private institution for breeding white people, enjoys a pre-eminent position in American culture. In lockstep with the function and power of white families, all designated black people are officially excluded from membership in white families. Some designated black people have biological family relations to members of white families, and, historically, their biological existence is a kind of fallout from the white breeding schema. Not surprisingly, both the exclusion and fallout began with the white exclusivity and white-imposed miscegenation that accompanied black slavery. W.E.B. Du Bois, in a 1908 study of the black American family, quoted a sister of President James Madison on this subject: "We Southern ladies are complimented with the names of wives; but we are only the mistresses of seraglios." Du Bois then quoted two white clergymen:

> Rev. Francis Hawley: As it relates to amalgamation, I can say, that I have been in respectable families (so-called), where I could distinguish the family resemblance in the slaves who waited upon the table. I once hired a slave who belonged to his own uncle. It is so common for the female slaves to have white children, that little or nothing is ever said about it. Very few inquiries are made as to who his father is. . . .
>
> Rev. Hiram White: Amalgamation was common. There was scarcely a family of slaves that had females of mature age where there were not some mulatto children.

Du Bois went on to quote the U.S. census: "Further proof of this is found in the statistics of mulattoes; the United States Census found 405,751 mulattoes in 1850, and 588,352 in 1860. These figures were, moreover, without reasonable doubt below the truth, as 'mulatto' was probably taken to mean a person, visibly at least half white. Probably one-fifth of the slaves in 1860 had distinct traces of white blood."[3]

After the abolition of slavery, although miscegenation caused by the sexual exploitation and coercion of black women by white men continued, deliberate statistics of individuals of mixed race were not consistently compiled, apart from counts of people who looked to be of mixed race and statistics of designated black children born "out of wedlock." However, contemporary geneticists speak of a race called "North American Coloured," said to have originated in the last few centuries and to be a mixture of Forest Negro, Bantu, and Northwest European. This new race, "North American Coloured," is coextensive with the group consisting of all designated black individuals in the United States.[4] By 1966 at least one study concluded that this group of "North American Coloured" contains 30 percent of the genes contained in the designated white population.[5]

The Black Concept of Physical Race and Black Families

The ordinary American concept of physical race has already been analyzed as a white ethnic concept. Due to the proscriptive kinship schema for breeding official white families, many designated black people have been excluded from and thrown out of white families. But black people also have an ordinary concept of physical race. What is the black ethnic concept of physical race, and how does it relate to black family structures?

At least since the days when miscegenation was the result of the sexual exploitation of black female slaves by white slave owners, there have been designated black Americans who look white. There have also been "mulattoes," "quadroons," "octoroons," and, in the other direction, "griffes." Both designated blacks and designated whites who have feelings of ethnic pride based on pure black or pure white racial identity may, at the least, feel uncomfortable with these words of mixed race. It is not clear whether these words are racist: If the words refer to designated race of forebears then they are no more racist than the words "black" and "white." But if the words refer to old "blood" theories of dilution in racial inheritance, then the words are extrinsically racist; and if "quadroons" and "octoroons" are believed to be superior to "mulattoes," "griffes," and presumed-to-be "pure" black people, then the words are intrinsically racist. The words could also be intrinsically racist if they are used to devalue designated black people who do not look "pure" black.[6]

In addition to the miscegenation imposed during slavery, the Africans who were brought to the United States as slaves did not all come from the same physical racial subgroups. Both miscegenation and differences in African origin have combined in myriad ways over the centuries to produce a greater variety of physical racial characteristics among designated black Americans than among designated white Americans.

Black Americans in general, and especially black Americans who value cultural tradition, apply the white asymmetrical kinship system with great rigor. According to "core" black standards, a person is black if he or she has one black forebear, no matter how white the person may look. And black Americans go one step further than white Americans in physical racial designations: If individuals who are darker in skin color than Nordic Anglo-Saxons— i.e., whites such as Italians, Hispanics, some Jews, Middle Eastern Semites, North Africans, and Indians—are accepted as physically racially white by whites on the basis of anthropological data and custom, this is not sufficient for blacks to accept that those individuals are white. Traditional blacks tend to view these groups of people, whom they call "munglas" (as opposed to "peolas," a word for fair-skinned designated blacks), as black people who are "passing" for white people.[7] It could be said that blacks, like intentional white racists, use the criterion of "blood in the face" for physical whiteness, although for blacks the ability to blush visibly is merely a necessary condition for physical whiteness and not a sufficient one. According to traditional ethnic (i.e., cultural) black concepts of physical whiteness, it is necessary and sufficient that an individual, A, have no non-white forebears, including non-whites whom whites do not designate as racially black, and that A have "blood in the face," for A to be racially white. Thus, not everyone who meets the criteria for whiteness among whites meets the criteria for whiteness among blacks.

Traditional black Americans do not, in general, think that those people who are designated white are superior to designated blacks. For example, John Langston Gwaltney's interviews of working-class urban blacks in the early 1970s document traditional black beliefs that whites are physically weak, greedy, deeply unethical, unable to act alone, stupid, and personally dirty. It may be ironic that these characterizations of whites bear a close resemblance to what used to be called "prejudiced" characterizations of blacks by whites. But it is not clear that these black stereotypes of whites were a simple reaction to white stereotypes of blacks.

Gwaltney's subjects and their relatives were reported to be generalizing their own experiences with white people. All of Gwaltney's subjects referred to lifetimes, going back for many generations to their foreparents' experience of slavery, of having been ill-treated by white people. These traditional black people believed that white people rule the world, based not on any superior abilities of whites compared to non-whites but due to the cruelty, greed, and ruthlessness of whites.[8] Traditional blacks see this as a moral matter—Gwaltney's subjects criticized whites on moral grounds—and are therefore extrinsic racists. Of course, there are also blacks who are intrinsically racist against whites, and they hold speculations about religious racial genealogy, black racial purity, and inherited racial traits and behavior, speculations which stand out as ideological, as do the racist speculations of white intrinsic racists.[9]

Gwaltney's subjects viewed the world as unjust and life as unfair. According to the principles of their most respected community members, great self-discipline and hard work were necessary for simple survival by black Americans. A traditional black person who held such views was said to be a "black person of the blacks."

A black person of the blacks cannot afford to be a hypocrite among blacks, and he or she has an obligation to instruct the young in the basic values of black culture.[10] For example, behaving properly toward designated black people who have been ill-treated by white intrinsic racists is an important traditional black virtue. In a more formal analysis than Gwaltney's interviews, one that criticizes traditional social science studies of the black family, Wade Nobles and Lawford Goddard insist that a very important function of the black family is to socialize children about how to deal with white racism.[11] This suggests that black family identity might be less stringently connected to "facts" of physical race than white family identity is.

Black people do not have a racial breeding schema that determines official black family membership. In general, blacks are quicker than whites are to categorize an individual as black based on a "nonwhite" appearance. But racial categories do not in themselves have moral values within black families. What does have a moral value in traditional black culture is how individuals whom blacks designate as black behave about their racial designations. It is assumed that if a person, B, would be thought black by blacks, then B must know that he or she is black; and if B accepts a white racial designation from whites, then although B's behavior might be understandable in terms of self-interest or self-preservation, B is nonetheless not to be trusted.[12]

Black people do not have to examine their family genealogies to make certain that they are black; nor do they have to control who is admitted into the family to protect the black racial identity of the family (although some black parents may not like it if their children marry whites and thereby undermine their ethnic identity).[13] It therefore seems reasonable to conclude that the ordinary concept of physical race for blacks is not strongly related to black concepts of black family identity, even though the black concept of physical race appears to be a more exclusive form of the white concept of white race, in favoring white racial purity.

Breeding

The white breeding schema of family identity is a form of social technology. When it is rigorously applied, it can result in people who look paradigmatically white according to white and black criteria (the latter being the more stringent). But the American white breeding schema has not kept the designated black race in America paradigmatically black in appearance. This is because black people have not had the option of rejecting those individuals with white forebears from their official families or wider social groups. And where there are individuals who appear to be paradigmatically black in the United States, it is not necessary for them to prove that they have no white forebears, because the presence of white forebears would not detract from their black racial designation. However, the absence of white forebears in their genealogies would be just as difficult for "pure" black people to prove as the absence of black forebears in their genealogies is for "pure" white people to prove. Furthermore, both "pure" white and "pure" black people in the United States could claim their racial purity only on the basis of family breeding and not on the basis of any inherent racial "essence." And breeding is a selective practice invented and reinforced within cultures. There is nothing that is natural about human breeding rules apart from the bare facts of human heterosexual reproduction.

The dominant white American racial caste is not the first caste in human society to maintain itself through selective breeding, but it may be one of the least self-conscious breeding castes in the whole of human history—to this day, most white Americans maintain the fiction that what they regard as races are natural kinds. This is probably because the Enlightenment ideals of individual freedom and heterosexual romantic love are consciously held by the dominant bourgeois class within this caste. And those ideals are at odds with the intrinsic and intentional racism and control over individuals that are required for the effective operation of the asymmetrical schema of white family identity, i.e., required to maintain white breeding.

The proscriptive white kinship schema reinforces and perpetuates ordinary ideas about physical races as natural entities. White men have traditionally exerted great control over family relations, within both their own and other people's families. There is no reason to think that the energy that for hundreds of years has gone into maintaining this control while the schema has been working would peacefully dissipate if the schema ceased to work in favor of whites. It could be argued that the repression of love that occurs when black offspring have been excluded from official white families—a repression that may be suffered by both designated blacks and designated whites and that is necessary to maintain the schema—is pathological. But few writers since Wilhelm Reich have tried to construct a theory about how presumably natural feelings of love for people who are close become converted into behavioral dispositions of domination and oppression.[14] It is doubtful that Reich's theories could be reclaimed in contemporary progressive thinking. However, until the mechanisms of white patriarchy are fully understood, to the point that it is known how to dismantle them, those who take action against white patriarchy on racial grounds will probably encounter violent counteraction. The history of white American violence against black men is as much a clue that American patriarchy must be white as it is a lesson against black-induced miscegenation.[15] And history has also taught that such violent responses and offenses are capable of coexisting, in the same white patriarchal individuals, with Enlightenment ideals of peace, rationality, and liberty: The coexistence is sheltered under the umbrella of "family values," which in this case means "white family values."

There are no exclusionary schemata for American black family membership, no foundations of black racial identity based on deep ontological negations. There is little, if anything, within black family structure that is analogous to the 'for-the-sake-of-the-family' concepts of physical racial identity found within white families. Members of black families thereby have more liberty to base family life on *biological ties*, bonds of love, and ethical obligations, if and only if—and this a large philosophical IFF—they can adjust to the economic and social hardships externally imposed on them by institutionalized white racism against blacks.

At this time in American history, designated American blacks are probably just as attached to the concept of physical race as are designated American whites. Whether blacks are separatist or assimilationist in their goals for their "black race," they still formulate these goals on the basis of physical races as natural kinds rather than as cultural effects of the white family breeding schema. This is clear on the surface of separatist discourse—if black people ought to separate from white society, then there must be some important independent basis, outside of the context of white racism, by which blacks can identify themselves.

Those blacks who favor racial assimilation through intermarriage, as, for example, E. Franklin Frazier did in 1939, speak of it as a form of progress for American blacks.[16] Since both American blacks and American whites, as conceptualized in American culture, are to a large extent the result of white breeding customs, which have been imposed on both groups, the concept of assimilation depends on the logically prior concepts of black and white physical race. If white breeding customs were no longer enforced, that is, if the preferred American family were no longer white, men and women would have children on whatever bases they have always had children, but no group of children would be more officially privileged than any other group.

There has already been widespread reproductive assimilation between designated blacks and designated whites. Black and white racial assimilation and miscegenation have been going on for hundreds of years in the United States. So people who speak of assimilation or miscegenation as either a terrible tragedy or a great hope are not referring to the possibility of anything new, in reality. The only practical question is how people whose existence is the result of miscegenation and assimilation should be designated and treated. If the children of miscegenation and assimilation are to be designated fairly and treated justly, what changes must occur in American culture?

5

Demography and the Identification of the Family

Wilhelm Reich's discussion of the sentimentalization and idealization of the patriarchal family by Third Reich propagandists offers some interesting general points about idealized family values. According to Reich, it may be in the interest of a fascist government to strengthen a form of the family which will support the imperialism of the state. But family values are presented to the public on emotional grounds, which include myths about a lost past and a fall from grace due to attacks on those values by certain designated or perceived enemies of the state.[1]

Many contemporary Americans place a high value on the family and on traditional family values that are believed to have been more prevalent in the past. But in our society, traditional family values have less to do with ancestral accomplishments than with an idealized model of family life. When this idealized model is accepted sentimentally and without criticism, moral goodness is automatically conferred on those who accept it. Although traditional family values are not legally and specifically protected by the government in American culture, criticism of the family is rare and not received with kindness, in general. Where feminists and traditional philosophers have neglected to defer to the necessity and goodness of the family, they have been chastised with bromides about ordinary people, the history of humanity, and commonly recognized obligations.[2] The core claim of this nostalgic criticism is that things are not as good outside the family as they were within it: Objects and services previously provided by families are of inferior quality when they are dispensed by public agency; love and care are better if they come from family members; sex and birth have a higher value within marriage (and so forth). The American family is also the basic earning and spending unit in an economic system that runs on consumption and credit.

However, no matter how hypocritical conventional praise of the American family may be, despite the dispensability of the family as a caring unit, in spite of the unhappiness of many marriages (and childhoods), and regardless of the commercial determinants of typical family forms, families are still the primary medium for bringing children from birth to maturity. In the United States and worldwide, the family is also the primary source of well-being and identity for individuals.[3]

As an economic and social unit and a source of well-being for individuals, American families are studied *demographically*: Measurements can be made of family size, family income, biological relations of family members, household accommodations, family health, illegitimate births, family educational levels, and so on. As a dimension of family life, demography is related to social class.[4] The higher the social class, the more successful the demographics of the family, e.g., more money, education, living-accommodation space, legal marriages, and so on. However, this is true only within a dimension of white or black race. Thus middle-class blacks have more successful demographics than lower-class blacks, and the same holds true for middle- and lower-class whites; but middle-class blacks might not have more successful demographics than lower-class whites.[5]

It is widely accepted that as a result of institutionalized racism against blacks, black families do not have the same norms and attainable ideals as white families. However, the equitable conclusion to be drawn from this disparity, namely, that black and white demographics ought not to be compared without qualifications that refer back to institutionalized racism, seems not to be as widely accepted. To be sure, social theorists who reject the white ethnocentric assumptions in American social science have argued forcefully for analyses of black family life that take the circumstances and values of black culture into account. But such arguments are

THE EXISTENTIAL ANALYSIS

often outside the mainstream of contemporary social theory—they are all too often presented in "Black Studies" contexts or forums that are polemically for or against "Afrocentricity."[6]

In addition to problems of bias in comparisons of black and white demographics, there is a more general conceptual problem with demographic studies of the American family, which while it may result in racial biases when demography intersects with race, does not itself seem to be based on any racial bias. This is the problem of the definition of the family in American bureaucracy, social science, and ordinary life. The family is defined as a unit of biologically related parents and children who live together. As Linda Nicholson indicates in her historical analysis of conceptions of the family, there have been times and places when the concept of family was not restricted to coresident, nuclear, biological relations. At different times in Western history, families have been variously organized and defined as broad kinship systems, "blood" lines of descent, and coresident groupings of kin and servants.[7]

One can imagine how people in the past who were not members of the dominant form of family organization felt about their deviation from the norm—this kind of deviation is a rich subject in contemporary art, literature, social science, and popular culture. But the problem with demography as a tool for studying families is not that it fails to document feelings of alienation but that it fails to document forms of family organization that are not the dominant form in a given culture. The contemporary American concept of the traditional family, nuclear or extended, became dominant in the nineteenth century.[8] If contemporary demographic studies of families are restricted by that culturally contingent form of family organization, and they tend to be, then such studies cannot tell us anything about other forms of family organization; nor can those other family forms be correlated with social and personal goods or ills. And the problem runs even deeper than this, on an ideological level: The dominant family form, or what is assumed to be the dominant family form, is taken to be the only morally good form of the family.

American social science has a long history of attempting to connect the problems of designated black Americans with the failure of the black American family to measure up to the dominant form of family organization.[9] Poverty, drug use, the commission of crimes, crime victimization, welfare dependence, and learning problems have all been interpreted by generations of social scientists as the effects of disorganized or dysfunctional black family life. The lack of black male heads of household, a lack which is traced back to the disruptive effects of slavery on black family life, is presumed to be the principal cause of these problems. In other words, black families are not sufficiently patriarchal and therefore, in a society that is organized into patriarchal family forms, all the other ills result.[10] However, black families cannot be sufficiently patriarchal because, due to racism, black men do not have the same opportunities to develop and function in society as white men do. Logically, this is a vicious circle: Black people are disadvantaged because they do not have the same kind of dominant families that white people have; black people do not have these kinds of families because they are disadvantaged. Meanwhile, black families, which are measured with the same demographic indicators that were derived from studies of the dominant family form— namely, a form that is typically exemplified by white families— are not perceived to be as good morally as white families.

It would help matters if all families could be first identified and then studied in ways that are neutral regarding dominant versus less-prevalent and less-preferred family forms. What is needed is a neutral definition of the family. Here are some questions that such a neutral definition might be expected to settle: Are kinship, coresidence, and legal marriage necessary for a group to be a family? Are deceased family members and divorced family members part of an individual's family? Are sexual relations necessary between individuals who are not related biologically for those individuals to be family members? If sexual relations are necessary, must they be heterosexual? Do family members have to be of the same race or culture? Must they have a common language? Can animals be family members of the families of human beings? Who has the authority to say, "No, there is no family here," or, "Yes, this is a family"? Can new forms of the family come into existence or even be deliberately invented? Must the family be defined as an objective, observable unit, i.e., *positivistically*, or can the family be defined in terms of individuals' concepts of their own families?

Here is a definition of the family, which would answer all of the questions that need to be settled by such a definition:

> *An individual's family are those sentient beings the individual feels most close to, thinks about most, and would suffer the loss of or separation from most grievously.*

This definition of the family makes necessary and sufficient conditions for family existence and family membership matters of choice and decision for individuals. Defined in this way, families are determined by the inner lives of individuals, and the family would always elude predetermined demographic parameters. This subjective concept of the family would preclude any ethnocentric evaluation of family forms—social scientists working from such a model of the family could not impose any preferred family structure on individuals and find those individuals lacking if they fell short of such a structure. If demographers wanted to study an individual's family, it would first be necessary to ask that individual who was felt to be closest, thought about most, likely to be missed most. If families are as important to individuals as everyone assumes they are, then why should not individuals (or communities or subcultures) be allowed to decide for themselves what families are and who anyone's family members are?

American demographic studies of family life tend to focus on coresidence or same-household membership. Family life is thereby defined as living in a house together. This definition is applied so literally that at least since the beginning of the twentieth century, house ownership has been the primary symbol of family life. W.E.B. Du Bois included forty-three photographs of houses in which Negro families lived in his 1908 study of the American black family. He spoke of "the needs of the American Negro home" and of "broken families."[11] To this day, some children with problems that are diagnosed by social scientists and other concerned people are referred to as "products of broken homes." Home ownership is not only a key demographic index but the primary symbol of American family life and a cherished value in the American "dream."

Contemporary Americans accept the connection between houses and families without question, on all levels of the culture. When demographers want to study family life, they go to people's houses, ring their doorbells, and ask them questions about the individuals who live in the houses. If not everyone who is supposed to be living in the house is there or if someone is there who is not supposed to be living in the house, then something is wrong with the family. So of course, it is reasoned backward that something must have been wrong with black families in the days of slavery because husbands and wives often had different owners, as did parents and children. But if one defines the family in terms of the inner lives of individuals, as suggested above, then such evaluations cannot be made. When spouses are separated against their will or children are taken away from parents, family members grieve because of the separation and loss. That they grieve shows that they have families, not that their homes have been broken or their families destroyed.[12]

In common language "a house is not a home," but in positivistic social science, which requires coresidence for family membership, and in a materialistic society that associates the goodness of family life with home ownership, a house is the physical expression of a home. Time spent in the house is home life, and home life is family life. However, on the basis of a subjective definition of the family, it is not clear where in space family life is lived, any more than it is clear where love, concern, and care are located in space.

By using positivistic criteria, such as same-household residence, for family membership, modern demography has created an artificial concept of a house as a mediating force between institutionalized white advantages (which make it easier for white families to own houses) and institutionalized black disadvantages (which make it more difficult for black families to own houses). The mediating concept of the house symbolizes a home. This home, which can be "broken" by the absence of a male "breadwinner" (another metaphor requiring clarification), is thus reified as a repository of the causes of black people's problems. If families were not defined as houses of individuals with patriarchs, then black families could not be viewed as the cause of black people's problems. Due to institutionalized racism, it is as difficult for black families to own houses as it is for them to have patriarchs (a difficulty that is exacerbated by racial discrimination in house sales).

This is not to suggest that people who are biologically or legally related ought not to live together in the same houses. The point is simply that family life is not coincident with coresidence or residence ownership. The nuclear, patriarchal, coresident family norm is contingent historically. In a mobile society, such as the present one in the United States, this form of the family has become only one possibility among many. The patriarchal, coresident, home-owning family is not the only family form legally permissible, morally worthy, socially beneficial, or economically productive; other family forms do not necessarily imply tragic or morally degenerate life "styles," and they are not automatically dysfunctional.

In the preceding two chapters, white racism against blacks was located in the ordinary concept of physical race. The tenacity with which people who are otherwise not racist cling to the concept of physical race was explained in terms of white family identity. Of course, white family identity, as racial identity, does not exhaust the meaning of family and family membership for white people. White racial family identity is simply a culturally contingent dimension of family identity in the United States. White family identity rests on unverifiable negations, and it can be easily destroyed by the recognized presence of black people in the family. But any racial family identity is not the same thing as family membership or family, in the subjective definition of family that has been proposed. Literature and biography yield many examples of white people with white family identities who nonetheless have had family ties with black people through love and kinship.[13] The mechanism of white family identity reduces to the approved breeding mores of white official families—that is, white families that are everywhere publicly recognized as white families and which enjoy the benefits of the privileged position of whites in comparison to blacks—a position that is currently called "institutionalized racism" (a term that also refers to the oppressed conditions of blacks).

There is no reason to believe that the mechanism of approved white breeding can provide a neutral definition of family or family membership any more than coresidence, patriarchy, or home ownership can. However, the problem with positivistic definitions as preferred foundations of the concept of family is a more general problem than the problem with racially privileged white-breeding concepts of family, even though the positivistic criteria may be deformed by racial criteria. The rejection of positivistic criteria for family identification—and, by extension, for individual identity—entails the rejection of white privileged criteria for family and individual identity. This is because lived family experience may elude the categories imposed by racial designations. But it should be stressed that there are reasons other than the restrictiveness or injustice of racial categories for rejecting positivistic criteria of the family. It has been shown, for example, that the failings of the coresidence requirement are a reason for rejecting positivistic definitions of the family.

THE EXISTENTIAL ANALYSIS

6

Mixed-Race Family Identity

nnette Baier, in her 1990 Presidential Address before the Eastern Division of the American Philosophical Association, pointed out that human beings come from families, born of women. She made it clear that it is necessary for this simple fact to be a philosophical subject, because the tradition of Western Philosophy, dominated by male philosophers, has privileged a concept of a person that is disembodied, culturally neutral, and ahistorical.[1] Feminist scholars such as Genevieve Lloyd and Susan Bordo have identified the disembodied person in Philosophy with the modern concept of rationality. This concept of a rational person was first constructed by René Descartes, to allow for that scientific distancing of the modern (masculine) mind from the modern (feminine) body.[2] The main philosophical point(s) here is that the traditional philosophical concept of a person is culturally relative (to the modern period), gender-biased (in favor of men), and inaccurate (as a description of ordinary life).

In the spring of 1991, Patricia Hill Collins warned a predominantly female (and white) audience that it is "dangerous" for those who are not white male academics to speak in voices that are neutral with regard to matters of class, race, and gender.[3] Patricia J. Williams, in an analysis of the hypocrisy of American legal ideals in *The Alchemy of Race and Rights*, published in 1991, insists that racial neutrality in the law merely provides a cover for racist implementations of the law.[4] The points made by Collins and Williams are a political message for women, non-whites, and "lower-class" intellectuals: Don't forget who you are, because if you do,

51

you will say and do things in your forgetfulness which will harm others who are what you are; identify yourself so that you will not be ignored or harmed under the guise of a false neutrality.

The Requirement of Personal Identification

Both the philosophical point and the political point, which have been expressed in myriad ways by scholars over the past two decades, have made it necessary to answer the question of personal identification, personally. A personal answer is now required in public from people who want to be heard on matters of class, race, and gender, because matters of class, race, and gender have not been discussed from the standpoint of "lower" class, non-white race, and female gender during most of the Western scholarly tradition. This requirement of a personal voice is a question of personal identification, and the respondent must determine who she is with reference to the past. There is a strong assumption behind this current question about identity that one is not the author of one's own class and race, which when they intersect with biological sex, give rise to gender (according to the current emancipatory paradigm).[5] So the question, "Who am I?" is really the question, "Who were they?" It is a question of family history.

The emancipatory requirement that all who would liberate and be liberated identify themselves through family history is believed to support *diversity*. The focus here is on those respondents whose family histories are different from the family histories of paradigmatic white male cultural leaders. No allowance is made for individuals who may be uncomfortable about sharing their family histories with strangers, for those who have no knowledge of their family histories, or for those whose family histories are so *different* that the dominant forms of family history do not apply. This suggests that the effort to resist and change the naive biases of a "view from nowhere" that favors traditional oppressors may sometimes make an informed view from nowhere desirable. This informed view from nowhere would presuppose the different points of view of all observers who can be categorized by race, class, and gender, as well as the points of view of those who cannot or do not wish to be so categorized.[6]

Family History and Genealogy

Philosophically, an informed view from nowhere is necessary to discuss some of the general structures of family history, or what is ordinarily understood as 'genealogy.' As unique and particular as everyone's family history is and as different as black American family history is from white American family history, without some sense of the general structures of family history there would be no commonly negotiable terrain to go by that name. For example, it seems self-evident that everyone has a linear genealogy of biological descent, whether or not each person knows exactly what it is.[7]

Although it was argued in Chapter 5 that the definition of the family should be left up to individuals, family history is constrained by biological relations. Thus an individual's family includes whomever that individual thinks about most, feels closest to, and would suffer the loss of or separation from most grievously—family is subjective. But an individual's family history or genealogy is a recordable chain of parents, grandparents, and great[n]-grandparents (where n is any degree of ancestry)—genealogy is objective. In European culture, this objectivity of family history means that it can be verified or corroborated by documentation, which is observable by persons other than the individual whose family history it is. Recorded family history can also be proved false, which makes it as scientific as any other form of historical inquiry.[8] (In non-European cultures, such as African cultures, which do not have written traditions, family history can still be objective, according to the standards of verification in oral traditions.)[9]

In European culture, the family histories of individuals are usually set out in diagrams called "family trees." Although family trees are private (insofar as the family is private), documented family trees and individual pedigrees have often been correlated with public and official records to establish inheritance claims, prove eligibility for marriage, and fulfill the obligations of religious affiliation.[10] But just as often, individuals study their own genealogies to develop their ideas of who they are—genealogy can be a strong component of personal identity.

The personal identity dimension of genealogy is not a neutral, factual matter but a dimension of family valuation and self-valuation. Somehow this kind of personal identity appropriates selected aspects of the past for value in the present. This personal identity dimension of genealogy becomes dynamic through narratives and "stories" from an individual's family history. These narratives and stories help an individual define the self for the self and identify that self for others, both within and outside of the individual's family.

Many people who do not believe in the inheritance of acquired human characteristics or memories nevertheless prize their family stories. In Western society, family stories have usually been considered the province of female family members, even to the extent of wives taking on the stories of their husbands' families from their mothers-in-law.[11] Not only are women the main tellers and keepers of family stories, but family stories are probably intricately bound up in the various political and economic complexities of female gender that are associated with the families of individuals. Thus, to the extent that family identity comes from family stories, it is subject to the power of women—to what used to be called their "sway"—in their traditional, private, and often oppressed roles. The objective sense of family history is preserved not in family stories but in government records, church records, and family Bibles, all of which are forms of documentation that have usually been administered by men in European history.

The objective documentation of family history is kept in the official public realm; it is an external record, which contains facts that lie outside of the lived reality of past family life as an individual imagines it. Family stories have their own records in the form of keepsakes, heirlooms, photographs, and diaries. But these records are informal and less conclusive than the external documentation provided by birth certificates, marriage licenses, death certificates, tax records, and wills. The external documentation not only is official and public but is a record of the intersection between the family and the larger community or government.

Within white American families, official documentation is normally accepted as a validation or confirmation of what is known about family history through family stories. There are occasional disturbances to this validation and confirmation: Previously accepted stories may be proved false, it may be learned that past family members had terrible diseases or were insane or criminal, illegitimacy may be disclosed, and so on. These types of discoveries are disturbances because people like to think well of past family members. Thinking well of past family members somehow helps individuals to think well of themselves. Even though people who belong to the major religions of Western culture glorify martyred and oppressed religious leaders of the past, they do not, in general, glorify past family members who were martyred and oppressed. (Also, those family members who were recorded as "failures," either in official documentation or in family stories, are not primary choices for individual identification.) When individuals do identify with past family members who were martyred or oppressed, the identification often creates a need to avenge or seek revenge for the tragic lives of those forebears. But, in general, the mores of white American family life allow some latitude in individual choices of whom to identify with from the history of one's family.

Black Family History and Slavery

All of the above structures of family history seem to be different in the histories of black families. To begin with, the average black American, although she may have an American ancestry that goes back further in time on American soil than the average white American, probably has a smaller amount of official documentation in her family history than the average white American. This is because black American families have not participated as fully in official public life as have white American families. Furthermore, the demographically recorded events in American family life are based on white norms. For example, there may have been fewer wills in black families because they owned less property than white families, and there were certainly fewer recorded deeds. There always have been fewer legal marriages, fewer contracts, shorter life spans, and greater poverty in black families; in recent history, there have been proportionally more black men than white men in prison, which further reduces opportunities to accrue laudatory official documentation in a society in which men earn public praise more often than women do.[12]

There is no reason to believe that black family stories are less capable of imparting meaning, affect, and personality to past family life as black people imagine it than are white family stories capable of imparting to white family life as white people imagine it. But the official documentation of the black stories is less likely to confirm or validate them and more likely to contain disturbances. Therefore, if family history is a combination of official documentation and family stories, one would expect a heavier reliance on family stories as a source of family history in black families than in white families. And because family stories are in the province of women, one would expect that black women would be more influential than black men in providing the material for identity which is based on family history. Individuals with black identities based on their families would thereby be twice "born of women." And if such individuals were mainly raised by their mothers, the matriarchal foundation of their identities would be further strengthened. In the context of a feminist critique of patriarchy, this might imply that there is greater individual freedom in black families—if matriarchs are less repressive than patriarchs. But the historical fact of slavery sharply curtails the liberty that blacks have in identifying with ancestors.

There were always free black people in the American colonies and then in the United States, throughout the period of slavery. However, although not all black people were slaves, all enslaved people were black by the time slavery became an institution.[13] Because the majority of black Americans were slaves during the period of slavery, it seems a reasonable assumption that most black American families have slave forebears.[14] Any black American thinking back through his or her family history as a source of iden-

THE EXISTENTIAL ANALYSIS

tity will have to face the probability of at least one slave forebear. If one identifies with a slave forebear or if one bases one's identity on having a slave forebear, that in itself is enough to create "identity problems" in a culture where other people are free to choose whether or not to identify with the oppressed and martyred individuals in their family histories. Furthermore, it is difficult not to identify with a black slave forebear for two reasons: First, the ordinary American concept of physical race entails that blackness is hereditary, and for a long time most black Americans were slaves; the second and more subtle reason is that in the United States, when slavery was legal, black people were slaves in perpetuity— the children of slaves were *born* slaves. The legal institution of slavery made slavery hereditary, and in general it was rare and difficult for individual black slaves to become free during the time of slavery.[15]

As a legal fact, the enslavement of individuals is the type of fact that would normally be part of a family's official documentation. It is a paradox that black slaves, qua property, did not have an official legal status in the contracts or bills of sale by means of which they were bought and sold.[16] A freed black person might have had manumission papers, but a slave did not carry around or pass on to descendants the documentation of her enslavement. If slavery is part of black family history, as a part of the history of any particular black family, it has been passed on through something more objectively verified than most family stories—i.e., History as a public subject—but certainly less accessible to genealogical searches by the concerned parties than all other kinds of official documentation. For example, in *Alchemy of Race and Rights*, Patricia Williams speaks of having come into possession of "what may have been" the contract of sale of her great-great-grandmother, Sophie, "a few years ago." It is clear that if this document came from family archives, they were not the archives of Patricia Williams's family. Indeed, Williams goes on to say that her sister found a county census record in which Sophie was listed among the "personal assets" of the man who owned her.[17] The question of who kept and who now controls the documentation of the important fact of slavery in black families is merely one more poisonous aspect of how slavery has a determining effect on American black identity.

The foregoing aspects of black family history presuppose a present point of view on the past. But suppose one imagines a slave ancestor looking forward. This ancestor would know that her children would be born slaves. She would know that the worst events of her life were likely to be repeated in the lives of her children. When the slaves were freed, why would former slaves think that the worst events of their lives were no longer inheritable, especially when those former slaves continued to occupy oppressed positions in society? Individuals who grow up in even the most privileged white families do not have the autonomy to choose which past family members to identify with, without first hearing what their parents tell them about who they are in the family context of identity. We all hear who our relatives think we are or of whom we remind them before we choose with whom to identify. How could it not be the case that a parent who was a slave or who had a parent who was a slave, when slavery existed in perpetuity, would not have a strong fear that being a slave would be part of who her child was? Does anyone think that children are unaware of their parents' fears for and about them? If identity is based on identification with past family members, is there any way that a black American who experiences racism in contemporary society can have an identity that is free of the fact of slavery? It seems unlikely. But the connection to the past must be passed on through family ties. And personal identification with the past through family ties is not a theoretical event.

It is not self-evident in theory that a state of slavery would be automatically inheritable. In the ancient world, the children of slaves were born slaves, just as in the United States. However, the memory of slavery was passed on within the family in the United States in ways that were probably not paralleled in the ancient world. In Rome, for example, manumitted slaves could become full citizens in a generation or two with no remaining social stigma.[18] The stigma attached to black slavery in the United States was (is?) due to the fact that only blacks were chattel slaves, plus the beliefs that blacks were an identifiable race and that their race was inheritable. In sum, slavery was made inheritable, all slaves were designated black, and blackness was made inheritable.

In theory, John Locke, who is said to have provided the basic ideals of American government, could have challenged the inheritability of slavery. Locke insisted that legitimate government required the consent of those governed because legitimate government existed to benefit those governed. As a corollary to this theory of government, Locke spoke of the limited rights of conquerors over the property and children of those conquered thus:

> But because the miscarriages of the father are no faults of the children, who may be rational and peaceable, notwithstanding the brutishness and injustice of the father, the father, by his miscarriages and violence, can forfeit but his own life, and involves not his children in his guilt or destruction. His goods which Nature, that willeth the preservation of all mankind as much as possible, hath made to belong to the children to keep them from perishing, do still continue to belong to his children.[19]

That is, if just conquerors have not conquered the children of those conquered, then someone who justly (or unjustly) enslaves people as a result of conquest ought not to have the right to enslave the children of those conquered. However, Locke did not argue against the inheritability of slavery or even against slavery itself. He referred to slaves as justly conquered captives who were not only outside of society but without property:

> But there is another sort of servant which by a peculiar name we call slaves, who being captives taken in a just war are, by the right of Nature, subjected to the absolute dominion and arbitrary power of their masters. These men having, as I say, forfeited their lives and, with it, their liberties, and lost their estates, and being in the state of slavery, not capable of any property, cannot in that state be considered as any part of civil society, the chief end whereof is the preservation of property.[20]

In both the ancient world and the United States, slaves were a form of property in the sense of material possessions. But according to Locke, the concept of property, which derived from an individual's ownership of his own body, did not mean merely property in the sense of material possession but property as a basic right, which included life, liberty, and estate, where the term 'estate' alone referred to property in the sense of material possession. Thus, after Locke has described the insecurity of human life without government, he says of that generic human being who is the subject of analysis:

> And it is not without reason that he seeks out and is willing to join in society with others who are already united or have a mind to unite for the mutual preservation of their lives, liberties and estates, which I call by the general name—property. The great and chief end, therefore, of men uniting in commonwealths, and putting themselves under government, is the preservation of their property; to which in the state of nature there are many things wanting.[21]

The inheritability of slavery is itself a perverse form of property in Locke's sense. The slave, who lacked property in the form of liberty and estate was compelled by law to pass on slavery to her descendants. It is as if slavery itself were some form of inalienable 'property.' It is as if in becoming property, in the sense of material possessions, slaves acquired *antiproperty* in the lack of liberty and material possessions combined. And unlike property in the sense of material possessions, the antiproperty of slavery was not something which slaves could alienate from themselves. It is interesting to note in this regard that it was impossible for Locke's generic subject to alienate his life or liberty (although for Locke, life and liberty were inalienable because they were given by God).[22]

Slavery in the form of material property was legitimized in the U.S. Constitution by delegates from non–slave-owning colonies at the Constitutional Convention in 1787. Slavery was accepted by all of the delegates because had it not been, the delegates from the slave-owning colonies would not have consented to become part of the new American government. Slavery was accepted on the grounds that slaves were the valuable and inalienable property of their owners.[23]

At any rate, in law the inheritability of black slavery had to do with the property (in the sense of material possessions) of slave owners. People who own property have interests in that property. In terms of property interests, more property is usually better than the same amount of or less property. The progeny of one's property is one form of more property if one owns living things. Since the ownership of one's property was a sanctified constitutional right as soon as there was a U.S. Constitution, one's ownership of one's slaves' children would be no different from the return on anything else one owned. It was in the property interests of slave owners that their slaves' children be born slaves. And given the value (and sanctity) of property, it would be in the slave owner's interest to overlook any degrees of racial mixture toward whiteness for as long as possible and into as many generations as possible. If there is a fear of miscegenation in the descendants of slave owners, it must at least in part be based on a habit of fearing miscegenation by slave-owning ancestors. But this is the miscegenation of black slaves, not of free white people. The miscegenation of black slaves could have, in theory, represented a dangerous dilution of capital to slave owners, not unlike the debasement of specie coin. That slaves could be capital, after all, was bound up with the fact that only black people could be slaves. And given the strong property interest in slavery, it does not seem farfetched to suggest that the "one drop" aspect of the inheritance of racial blackness (discussed in Chapters 2 and 3) had its roots in the strong property interest that slave owners had in the inheritance of slavery.

Slave and Slave-Owning Family History

The interests of slaves were strongly opposed to the interests of slave owners, even if slaves and slave owners were members of the same biological family. And the descendants of such slave and slave-owning biological families would have contradictory identities, depending on whether they identified with a slave or a slave-owning ancestor. To have a family history which includes both slave and slave-owning members and to know something about both types of forebears could only create havoc within any identity based on family history. And this is probably the paradigm case of American mixed black and white identity that is based on family history, when the individual thinks back through the family to slavery.

There have always been designated black Americans who knew that they had both slave and slave-owning forebears. It would seem that, traditionally, their racial identity is based on identification with the past family members who were slaves, if they think back that far into their family histories. To begin with, there was no choice in this matter by law until, at most, the last twenty-five years in some southern states—miscegenation laws were first struck down by the U.S. Supreme Court in 1967;[24] and the custom of the asymmetrical kinship schema of racial inheritance, or the one-drop rule, forces such an identification. Furthermore, it is probably more tranquil psychologically not to identify with both a slave and a slave-owning ancestor; to do so could be *schizophrenigenic*.

In *Alchemy of Race and Rights*, Patricia Williams diagnoses herself as schizophrenic when she recounts visions of archetypal polar bears during a winter break in which she attended back-to-back academic conferences on literature and on law. This is Williams's description of her symptoms of schizophrenia:

> I sleep fitfully in the New Orleans humidity. I dream that I'm teaching my Uniform Commercial Code class. My students are restless and inattentive, bored to death with the sales of chattels. Suddenly, from somewhere deep in my psyche, polar bears rise. Silent, unbidden, they come to the dissolved walls of the classroom, the polar bears come padding to hear what this law will mean for them. It is snowing in their world. Hunching, they settle at the edge of the classroom, the walls of the classroom melt in the heated power of their breath, their fierce dark eyes are fixed upon me. They hunch and settle and listen, from beyond-language.
>
> I wake up in a cold sweat.
>
> I wake up. Yet large eyes still gleam inquiringly from the foot of the bed. The eyes at the foot of the bed are larger than flashlights. They are polar-bear eyes. I am terrified. (Why am I so terrified? Some part of me knows that it is intelligent for me to be schizophrenic . . .)[25]

Later Williams offers her reader a story about polar bears from her childhood:

My mother's cousin Marjorie was a storyteller. From time to time I would press her to tell me the details of her youth, and she would tell me instead about a child who wandered into a world of polar bears, who was prayed over by polar bears, and was in the end eaten. The child's life was not in vain because the polar bears had been made holy by its suffering. The child had been a test, a message from god for polar bears. In the polar-bear universe, she would tell me, the primary object of creation was polar bears, and the rest of the living world was fashioned to serve polar bears. The clouds took their shape from polar bears, trees were designed to give shelter and shade to polar bears, and humans were ideally designed to provide polar bears with meat.[26]

After a brief discussion of rights, personal identity, and empowerment, the reader is told of a "lovely polar-bear afternoon," and then, "In the newspapers the next day, it was reported that two polar bears in the Brooklyn Zoo mauled to death an eleven-year-old boy who had entered their cage to swim in the moat. The police were called, and the bears were killed." The reader learns that this mauled child had been "born into the urban jungle of a black welfare mother and a Hispanic alcoholic father who had died literally in the gutter only six weeks before."[27]

Williams ends her book on this note:

I allowed myself to be watched over by bear spirits. Clean white wind and strong bear smells. The shadowed amnesia; the absence of being; the presence of polar bears. White wilderness of icy meateaters heavy with remembrance; leaden with undoing; shaggy with the effort of hunting for silence; frozen in a web of intention and intuition. A lunacy of polar bears. A history of polar bears. A pride of polar bears. A consistency of polar bears. In those meandering pastel polar-bear moments, I found cool fragments of white-fur invisibility. Solid, black-gummed, intent, observant. Hungry and patient, impassive and exquisitely timed. The brilliant bursts of exclusive territoriality. A complexity of messages implied in our being.[28]

Williams is clearly suggesting that the polar bears in her psyche are her white ancestors. The reader knows that Williams's great-great-grandmother, Sophie, was purchased at age eleven by a white lawyer, who immediately impregnated her. That was the beginning of the designated black family whose history furnishes Williams with her identity based on family history.[29] Williams is a law professor. Before she began her studies at Harvard, her mother encouraged her to feel confident about studying law by telling her that the law was "in [her] blood," because the man who had impregnated Sophie was a lawyer, as were many members of his white family. This white family of lawyers was part of Patricia Williams's family as well—Sophie's child by her white owner was Patricia Williams's great-grandmother.

Williams's poetic analysis of the legal rights and practical nonrights (and perhaps antirights) of black people succeeds as a description of how the law works and does not work for contemporary black Americans. It is not clear that she also succeeds in presenting a sense of identity based on past family members who were both slaves and slave owners. Her presented identity is not a deliberate, rational construction but a discourse of her psyche, which cannot be fully conveyed in words—one has to share the image of predatory white polar bears who are a part of the very self they terrify. Williams's reader can only marvel at the orchestration of literature and legal analysis out of what might otherwise be incommunicable insanity. If the reader can let go of words in response to Williams's artistry, she may be reminded of the chorale movement of Ludwig van Beethoven's Ninth Symphony, which celebrates the union of what "stern custom has kept apart." (Indeed, this association is supported by Williams's discussion of the belief in American black culture that Beethoven himself was a mulatto.)[30] However, on a conceptual level Williams has not done more than hint at deep problems of self-identity and self-identification when these are based on designated black family history.

To return to the philosophical and political requirements that identity be connected with family history, it is now clear that the form of black family history is inherently problematic in comparison with the form of white family history. Not only does black family history contain self-undermining recollections of being oppressed, but its racial diversity may lead a descendant to an irreconcilable slave and slave-owning genealogy. If one would liberate oneself through identification by means of family history, one may also have to liberate one's ancestors. Indeed, the contemporary scholarship about American slave lives, which documents the ways in which slaves nurtured their humanity in situations of extreme oppression, does just that. But freeing one's own slave ancestors through such scholarship is only part of the reclaiming task in contemporary liberating projects of American black identity. If designated black Americans are not racially pure—and most are not—then individual attempts to identify the self on a foundation of family history, where the individual identifies with black forebears, will be seriously frustrated by the presence of oppressive white forebears. Designated black Americans who are racially mixed and who identify with their white ancestors will face a different problem of accepting as part of their identity black ancestors who have been devalued by white ancestors. And of course, black Americans who identify with black ancestors and black Americans who identify with white ancestors share the problem of accepting black forebears who have been devalued by the white culture at large. There is no clear way around these obstacles.

In sum, the American problem of mixed race creates crises of personal identity if personal identity must be based on individual family histories. A person of mixed black and white ancestry might thereby be motivated to investigate the possibility of a mixed-race identity based on impersonal historical facts about people of mixed race in the United States. To be sure, there are more abstract, theoretical reasons to investigate this history of mixed race. But the demand for self-identification and the need for self-identity in current emancipatory discourse impart autobiographical relevance to those theoretical problems of biracialism that might otherwise fully justify such a historical investigation.

II

THE HISTORY of MIXED RACE

7

Introduction
to the History of
Mixed Race

R eceived opinion holds that racial identity is a good thing to
have: Knowledge about one's "own people" enriches an
individual life, it is good to know *what* one is. This racial
identity is usually based on the past, and family history is a normal
starting point. However, the attempt to base mixed-race identity on
family history more likely than not will fail against the realities of
the American biracial system. A biracial society does not, in general, support the formation of mixed-race families. And in any
particular case, the facts of a mixed-race lineage may be associated
with personal trauma and tragedy. Furthermore, individuals who
are the first "issues" of mixed race in their families do not have
any forebears of mixed race with whom they can identify.

The difficulties with family-history foundations for mixed-race
identity lead to the question of whether an identity of mixed race
can be based on the impersonal history of mixed race in the United
States. The purpose of this part is to explore that possibility.

The impersonal history of a person as a member of a racial group
would include biography (individual life histories), the officially documented history of the group, and the histories of other racial groups
as they intersect with the group under study. In the last sense, impersonal racial history includes general, public history made up of law
and custom. The culture of a racial group—its art, literature, and
music—and its depiction in the cultures of other racial groups
would be interwoven with the official documentation.

To undertake an investigation of the history (or sociology or
psychology) of a racial group implies that racial groups are real,

69

monolithic entities. Few writers today are entirely comfortable with that implication, so disclaimers about the false concept of physical race are common, especially in the social sciences. For example, in *New People*, which is presented as the first book-length study since 1918 of American mulattoes and miscegenation, historian Joel Williamson writes:

> In writing this book, it has seemed useful to preserve the flavor of the thinking of past times by occasionally using the terms the people themselves used in the way they used them. For example, in the past people often thought that character and culture were carried, quite literally, in the blood. Thus they would sometimes characterize persons of mixed ancestry as having "mixed blood," meaning to suggest a cultural as well as a physical mixture. There has also existed a folk concept of race. Scientific scholars generally agree that there is actually no such thing as race, that mixing has been universal and perpetual and that human traits so overlap that it is impossible to describe the characteristics of one "race" to the exclusion of all others. These scholars prefer to think in terms of a "gene pool" that produces certain traits among an inbred people more frequently than among others. What seem to be races, one might say, are actually clusters of traits. But even though blood did not itself carry character and culture, and, scientifically, races did not really exist, I will sometimes speak as if they did.[1]

Contra Williamson, it should be possible to discuss the history of mixed race without using the concept of blood as a carrier of cultural traits. This concept is still too closely associated with old theories of race to function as a metaphor, and any 'reality' in the concept is dissipated by the common knowledge that, to put it crudely, blood transfusions are not vehicles for cultural change. It has already been argued that races do not exist in the sense in which reasonable people persist in speaking as if they did (see Chapter 2). If races do not exist, then mixed races do not exist either; and since neither races nor mixed races exist, black, white, and mixed black and white people do not exist. But, of course, people exist who designate themselves and others in these ways. In the United States, racial words are so commonly used that one

THE HISTORY OF MIXED RACE

must not only mention them but use them in order to understand important human activities.[2] That is perhaps the justification implicit in Williamson's disclaimer. However, using the words of race is nothing so quaint as preserving the "flavor of the thinking of past times" (as Williamson puts it) but is a vital tool of the kind of cultural understanding that requires participation in the culture under study. (By way of example, there are now anthropologists who insist that foreign cultures can be understood only if the observer learns the language as an infant learns it and not as a student with a dictionary and interpreter might learn it.)

My intention here is to use the words "race," "mixed race," "black," "white," "mulatto," "quadroon," and so on as an anthropologist might use the words "untouchable," "berdash," "totem," "shamin"—the words are used to describe what is going on in a culture, in order to understand that culture.[3] But, unlike an anthropologist, a philosopher goes beyond understanding into analysis. The analysis translates the understanding of how racial words are used into a theory or worldview, which is then criticized. A philosopher who also likes words could call this use of racial words a "critical, philosophical, anthropological analysis"—and, in this case, it would also be "historical."

Suppose it is possible to practice critical, philosophic anthropology on one's own culture. Isn't such a practice an exercise in intellectual arrogance, which imitates the practices of white, male, ethnocentric European intellectuals? Not necessarily. For example, there is a tradition of philosophic anthropology in African village life, and a subset of that tradition is critical.

Henry Odera Oruka writes about the folk practice of philosophy in Africa to back up his claim that there is a discipline of African Philosophy that is more than Western Philosophy imitated by Africans, and which is distinct from Ethnocentric African Ideology and African Nationalism. According to Oruka, African sages who rigorously use logic, reason, and scientific curiosity meet the requirements of philosophers in a universalist sense. Oruka distinguishes between two types of African sages: There are sages who are versed in the wisdom and traditions of their people and who function as moralists, historians, and interpreters of customs; and there are sages who are knowledgeable in the first sense and, in addition, are rationally critical thinkers who recommend only those aspects of the communal culture which satisfy their "rational scrutiny."[4] I would say that the second type of African sage, who scrutinizes the mores of his people, is practicing a critical, philosophic anthropology in the way I will try to do here. Obviously, Oruka's sage is not European because he is African; nor is he ethnocentric, because he criticizes his own tradition. This type of sage works purely in an oral tradition, and although the sage is typically male, he need not be sexist—Oruka quotes a Luo sage who argues that men and women "are naturally equal or balanced"![5]

Proceeding from Oruka's paradigm, although racial words may need to be used, they need not be used uncritically. Therefore the following caveat is in keeping with a critical, philosophic analysis of the history of mixed race in the United States: *The terms referring to the chiaroscuro of individuals between black and white make better sense if one thinks of these terms as referring to the races of an individual's forebears, rather than to the race of that individual.*

This caveat is another way of saying that you cannot tell the race of a designated non-white individual's forebears by looking at that individual. It was explained in Chapter 2 that the racial characteristics of forebears are not present in predictable fractions in any individual offspring. This is a reference to the Mendalian laws of heredity (which have not been disproved by biologists).[6] For example, suppose an individual, X, has one black grandparent and three white grandparents. One of X's parents will be a mulatto, i.e., will have one-half of the black genes. Because each individual gets one-half of all her genes from each parent, X might have any—up to one-half—of the black grandparent's racial genes, and X might have all, none, or some of the mulatto parent's black racial characteristics.

Alternatively, suppose we begin with X and note that X has very dark skin and very "Negroid" facial features. X could have two mulatto parents and two Nordic grandparents. That is, it could be the case that X got her appearance because all of the black characteristics of both of her parents combined at her conception.

In general, the customary language of mixed race designates an individual as one-quarter black if that individual has one black grandparent. But since there is ordinarily no way to know that X does have one-quarter black genes out of four-quarters total racial genes, it would be more precise to refer to X as a person with one black grandparent than as a person who is one-quarter black. A person who would customarily be called one-eighth black would be more precisely designated as someone with one black great-grandparent.[7] Until all human genes have been mapped, that is, identified and correlated with specific perceptible human characteristics, and until the genes of any one individual can all be identified, it is impossible to tell what racial genes any individual has, with any scientific precision.[8] Finally, it should be kept in mind that although such complete genetic mapping is, in principle, possible, if it were accomplished it would not make concepts of race more scientific but merely allow for greater precision in how people applied their nonscientific concepts of race.

As is discussed in Chapter 8, the history of individuals of mixed black and white race in America goes back to the early 1600s. However, as of now Americans of mixed black and white race do not have an *identity* as mixed-race individuals in law or society, and they never have had such an identity in the official or public, legal, and social history of the United States. It is difficult to understand how odd this situation is without stepping back from the American cultural context to sketch the logic of a neutral situation of mixed race.

There is no scientific or empirical basis for the existence of races such that any race consists of a set of defining physical characteristics that are present in every individual who is a member of that race. But suppose there were such a physical thing as the race of a person; and suppose, for example, that an individual, S, had a parent of P race and a parent of Q race. Then S would be mixed P and Q race. Suppose further that neither P traits nor Q traits dominated the other in heredity, so that in appearance and in whatever else was taken to be "racial," as far as anyone could tell, S really was a mixture of P and Q in hereditary endowment.[9] Then if S, who was P–Q, mated with R, who was pure Q, it would seem safe to assume that the offspring of S and R—say, T—would be more Q than P, although still of a P–Q mixture.

If the society in which P's and Q's lived were value-neutral about P and Q, then S and T, as mixtures of P and Q, might privately decide that they were both P and Q or that they were perhaps a different race, O. If racial designations were important for some reason (albeit still value-neutral), then individuals such as S might insist that the "authorities" recognize the existence of O. Alternatively, T's, who were more Q than P, might shrug and call themselves Q's. There might also be U's, the offspring of P–Q's and P's, who were more P than Q, and these U's might call themselves P's or insist on a new racial designation N. At any rate, it would be possible, if society were neutral regarding P and Q, to speak of individuals who were mixed P and Q, and to leave it up to those individuals to support research into their own new racial characteristics and ultimately make a decision about how, as individuals of mixed race, they wished to be regarded racially. If racial categories were important for some reason, and if a society were neutral about them and there were a fair degree of freedom and self-determination in that society, then that might be the dynamic of racial change.

Even if society favored P or Q and were not neutral about matters of race, one can still imagine that it might be possible for racially mixed individuals to have racially mixed identities. Indeed, history is replete with examples of this type of situation. In South Africa, for example, a country notorious for favoring its white minority and the white race over the black race, there is a racially intermediate category of individuals who are called "colored."[10] In India during British rule, people who had both Indian and British parents were designated "out-castes," or "Anglo-Indians," and recognized as a distinct racial group both by Indians and by the British.[11] In Brazil the black race is devalued in comparison with the white race, but anyone with known white ancestry is recognized as "not-black," with the attendant opportunity of upward mobility through white-controlled society.[12] In the United States, however, there has never been a recognized category of mixed black and white race. Individuals with both black and white forebears have always been considered black, both legally and socially, in the contexts of both white and black society.

It is understandable that white people who wanted to perpetuate as many slaves as possible would insist that all people of mixed race were black.[13] It is also understandable that white people who simply believed that white people were racially superior to black people might want to take care to exclude people of black ancestry from the socially designated white race. But it is not as clear on the face of it why a black person, in the absence of racial neutrality, would want to impose a black designation on a racially mixed person. The more racially white any designated black person appears to be, the more the black racial designation of that person enforces the social devaluation of the black race. For anyone to insist that an individual be designated black solely on the strength of the racial designation of that individual's forebears merely enforces the idea that blackness is so terrible that neither individual identity, nor biological reality, nor generations of hereditary distance can erase it.

It has been estimated that between 70 and 80 percent of all designated black Americans have some degree of white ancestry.[14] If Americans, like Brazilians, were racist but more benevolent toward individuals, then 70 to 80 percent of all designated black Americans could be redesignated not-black. This is not to suggest that such redesignation would alleviate the problems of black Americans—the traditions of racial discrimination are too powerful in American life for any mere linguistic change to erase the kinds of racism that are an integral part of American life. (And resistance to the suggestion that American racial categories be redrawn might underscore the earlier claim that American racial categories are themselves racist—see Chapters 1 and 2.)

The historical facts of American mixed racial identity continually reiterate the exclusive, disjunctive racial system in the United States. An analysis of these historical facts will form the topics of Chapters 8 through 13 as follows. Chapter 8: The legal imposition of blackness on individuals who were of mixed race was effected from the early 1600s on by white legislators, judges, juries, and social leaders. This legal history consists both of laws against miscegenation in the American colonies and states and of varied definitions of blackness and whiteness. Chapter 9: There have been exceptions to the biracial American system in the form of mixed racial communities, many of which eventually died out, but E. Franklin Frazier's classic account of these "racial islands" is biased toward patriarchy. Chapter 10: From the Harlem Renaissance of the 1920s on, the designation of people of mixed black and white race as solely of black race was taken up by black people and previously designated people of mixed race. Thereafter mixed black and white racial identities were explored within the designation of the black racial category or within the wider context of black racial identity as circumscribed by whites. Chapter 11: The phenomenon of mixed race has been a varying topic in political discussions, social essays, and scientific speculations. In these contexts Americans of mixed race have been presented as victims of a cruel system, leaders of the black race, and physical and moral degenerates, as well as a danger to both black and white people who are racially pure. Chapter 12: Fictionalized characters of mixed race have reflected all of the roles discussed in Chapter 11, with the added dimension of black racist condemnation by black writers. Chapter 13: The foregoing impersonal history of mixed race adds up to a complex form of alienation that appears to be radically different from other forms of alienation experienced by oppressed people.

8

The Law
on Black and White

*I*n *Loving v. Virginia* in 1967, the U.S. Supreme Court unanimously struck down all remaining laws against interracial marriage and sexual relations. Mildred Loving was black and her husband, Richard, was white. They had been married for nine years and had three children whom they wanted to raise in the community in Virginia where they had grown up.[1] Besides Virginia, fifteen other states had miscegenation laws in 1967: Alabama, Arkansas, Delaware, Florida, Georgia, Kentucky, Louisiana, Mississippi, Missouri, North Carolina, Oklahoma, South Carolina, Tennessee, Texas, and West Virginia.[2]

At one time or another before 1967, thirty-eight states had laws against marriage between blacks and whites.[3] As a result of these laws, all individuals of mixed race who were born in those thirty-eight states were illegitimate: The laws against miscegenation did not stop the occurrence of interracial heterosexuality or the birth of individuals of mixed race. What the laws did accomplish was the imposition of bastardy, or illegitimacy, on such individuals. Throughout most of American history, most individuals of mixed race were the children of interracial sex between white southern men and black women, and the laws against interracial marriage were not intended to criminalize those relations.[4] The concubinage of black women by white men was tolerated in the same places where the miscegenation laws existed. Not tolerated were sexual relations between black men and white women or, in general, legal marriage across racial lines. In 1944, Swiss sociologist Gunnar Myrdal summed up the American attitude toward miscegenation in this frequently cited passage from his study of American race relations: "The astonishing fact is the great indifference of most white Americans toward real but illicit miscegenation. . . . The illicit relations freely allowed or only frowned upon are, however, restricted to those between white men and Negro women. A white woman's relation with a Negro man is met by the full fury of anti-amalgamation sanctions."[5]

As James Kinney remarks, *amalgamation* is an interesting trope in American letters and rhetoric.[6] The word came from metallurgy where it meant the mixture of a metal with mercury. Etymologically, "amalgamation" derives from the Greek *malagma*, which meant an emollient or, literally, "an application that softens living animal textures." The trope is interesting because its background is sufficiently man-made and nonorganic to connote something unnatural to human beings. But this trope did not appear in colonial sanctions against miscegenation. During the colonial period, American ideas about race had not yet themselves been amalgamated. It required the pressures of the American Revolution; the full-blown institution of plantation slavery; the Civil War; Reconstruction; and varied oppressive elements of frustration, revenge, hatred, and spite to solidify the racist compounds of American ideals of racial purity.

In 1619 twenty African slaves were purchased in Virginia and used to cultivate the tobacco crop. These early slaves were set to work side by side with white European indentured servants. Children of mixed race were born soon thereafter. The fathers of some of these children were white slave traders in Africa and seamen from the Middle Passage, but miscegenation also occurred frequently within the combined slave and indentured-servant laboring class.[7]

In 1630 there was a Jamestown court order that "a white man by the name of Hugh Davis, . . . be soundly whipped before an assemblage of negroes and others for abusing himself to the dishonor of God and the shame of Christians by defiling his body in lying with a negro, which fault he is to acknowledge next Sabboth [*sic*] day."[8] In 1662, Virginia enacted the first law prohibiting interracial marriage. Although the most frequent interracial sex was between white men and black women, the children of these unions were not relegated to their fathers in the tradition of British patriarchy but were given the status of their mothers.[9] The mixed-race children of white women were not slaves, but they were often bound to indentured servitude well into their adult years. The white mothers of such children also had their own periods of servitude extended, and they were subject to fines and other legal penalties. In 1691, Virginia enacted a law requiring that any free white woman bearing a mulatto child had to pay a fine within thirty days or face indentured servitude for five years for herself and thirty years for her child. The child, "that abominable mixture and spurious issue," was to be *sold* as a servant.[10]

In 1705 the Virginia assembly decreed that any minister who married a racially mixed couple had to pay a fine of ten thousand pounds of tobacco.[11] Eventually it became illegal for mulattoes to marry blacks in Virginia. However, in 1715 mulattoes were allowed to testify in court, and they could be punished as if they were white when convicted of crimes.[12] Maryland was more stringent than Virginia. In 1664 any Maryland woman who married a Negro slave had to serve her husband's owner for the rest of her married life. It was further stipulated that the "Issue of such freeborne woemmen soe marryed shall be Slaues as their fathers were."[13] In Pennsylvania a general miscegenation law prohibited interracial union of all kinds and condemned the mulatto children of white women to indentured servitude for thirty-one years.[14] Between 1705 and 1725, most of the other colonies passed laws similar to those in Virginia, Maryland, and Pennsylvania. However, despite the proscriptive legislation, it has been estimated that by the time of the Revolution there were between 60,000 and 120,000 people of mixed black and white race in the American colonies. The official U.S. census counted the total black population as 757,000 in 1790, although there was no official count of mixed-race individuals until 1850.[15]

The total American population was four million at the most in 1790, so the mixed-race segment of that population was at most a minority of 3 percent.[16] Nonetheless, people of mixed race were perceived to be a problem throughout the period of colonial legislation. Although not all colonials of mixed race were slaves or indentured servants, in legislation the free people of mixed race were listed in sequence with "servants, negroes, slaves, mustees and Indians."[17] In 1691 the Virginia assembly voted to discourage additional manumissions by forcing slave owners to send freedmen out of Virginia. In the same legislation, officials were encouraged to break up bands of Negroes, mulattoes, and other slaves who "lie, hide and lurk in obscure places." By 1723 free mulattoes were deprived of the right to vote, their possession of firearms was limited, and free mulatto women were discriminately taxed.[18]

During the Revolution, the free Negro population, which was previously only 20 percent black, became 60 percent black as the emancipation of blacks and mulattoes increased in the upper South. It became necessary at that time to define a Negro legally. Most upper southern states followed the lead of Virginia: According to Virginia law, a Negro was a person who had one black grandparent. This definition created a segment of the white population that was legally white but black in appearance or known ancestry.[19] But the legal whiteness of individuals of mixed race rarely protected them from the harsher designations made by custom. In time, all of the advantages of legal whiteness that accrued to individuals of known mixed black and white race gave way to the condemnation in the one-drop rule, although for different reasons in different places.

Joel Williamson notes that according to the 1859 census, there were 406,000 individuals of mixed race out of a total black population of 3,639,000. Approximately one-third of the mixed-race population, or 159,000, were free. One-half of the persons of mixed race, generically called "mulattoes," were in the upper South, the states of Virginia, Kentucky, Missouri, Maryland, Delaware, North Carolina, Tennessee, and the District of Columbia. Another one-third of the mulatto population was in the lower South, the states of Florida, Texas, South Carolina, and Louisiana. The rest of the mulatto population was mainly in New York and Pennsylvania, although small numbers were scattered evenly throughout the other states. In 1850 all of the mulattoes outside of the upper South and the lower South were free.[20]

In the upper South about 37 percent of all mulattoes were free, and they made up 35 percent of the total free Negro population. In the lower South the free mulattoes were 75 percent of the free Negro population and 17 percent of the total mulatto population. Williamson develops the thesis that, as a general rule, the older the slave-owning settlement, the greater the number of free mulattoes. Thus in the old slave states of Delaware, Maryland, Virginia, and North Carolina half of the mulattoes were free, and in the new slave states of Georgia, Mississippi, Arkansas, Alabama, Florida, and Texas only about 6 percent of the mulattoes were free.[21]

By 1850 the status of free mulattoes varied greatly. In Georgia, a relative newcomer to slavery that functioned as a frontier, free mulattoes had all the rights of whites, except for voting and sitting in the assembly. Throughout the lower South, free mulattoes tended to be recognized by whites as an intermediate caste between whites and blacks, perhaps because there were fewer whites in proportion to black slaves in the lower South. In Louisiana and South Carolina, many free mulattoes were prosperous: They owned both land and slaves, accumulated wealth, and were successful artisans, tradespeople, professionals, and artists.[22] During the entire period of slavery in South Carolina, there was no law against racial intermarriage.[23] Under the French Napoleonic Code in Louisiana, most mulattoes had been free because children took the status of their fathers. But in 1832 the Louisiana courts, under American law, ruled that the children of slave mothers were to be slaves.[24]

In the upper South, free mulattoes were associated with their lower-class white colonial forebears, and they tended to be marginal both economically and legally.[25] Throughout the rest of the United States, mulattoes had the same disadvantages as in the upper South because they were grouped with blacks as a whole. Rarely anywhere did mulattoes have suffrage.[26]

The tolerance toward mulattoes in the antebellum South was eroded by three forces: King Cotton, the defeat of the South in the Civil War, and white southern racism, which amalgamated after Reconstruction. From 1830 on, when cotton reigned, there were fewer manumissions of all slaves. Sometimes both freedom and property were bequeathed to mulatto kin in a master's will, but in many documented court cases, white heirs successfully intervened and the mulatto heirs were both disinherited and sold as property.[27] Between 1850 and 1860 the mulatto slave population increased by 66.9 percent, while the black slave population increased by only 19.8 percent. It was no longer legal to import slaves by this time, and Virginia and Kentucky were primary suppliers of new slave labor to the frontier slave states. As slavery became increasingly "whiter," the one-drop rule became more important as a justification for the existence of many slaves with light skin. (It was assumed that a white person could not be a slave.)[28]

During the 1850s the white tolerance of free mulattoes in Louisiana disappeared almost overnight in the face of northern abolitionist polemics. Vigilante violence erupted in attempts to drive wealthy free Negroes out of the state. By 1854, Henry Hughs of Mississippi was able to argue that "hybridism is heinous" and receive an enthusiastic white response to the following statement: "Impurity of races is against the law of nature. Mulattoes are monsters. The law of nature is the law of God. The same law which forbids consanguinous amalgamation forbids ethnical amalgamation. Both are incestuous. Amalgamation is incest."[29]

In 1856 a judge in Louisiana could still declare, "there is . . . all the difference between a free man of color and a slave, that there is between a white man and a slave."[30] But in 1857 it became illegal for mulatto slave children to be emancipated in Louisiana.[31]

During Reconstruction there was a brief time when a small number of marriages and love affairs between white women and black men were accepted in communities in Alabama and Louisiana. But, in general, once all Negroes had been freed, whites grew more inclined not to recognize categories of mixed race. Miscegenation between blacks and whites fell off sharply after the Civil War, although miscegenation between mulattoes and other blacks led to a doubling of the mulatto population between 1860 and 1890 and to an increase of 81 percent in that population between 1890 and 1910.[32] These racial mixtures reflected the increasing tendency of mulattoes to identify with blacks as a whole,

THE HISTORY OF MIXED RACE

rather than to see themselves as a separate group. Indeed, mulattoes as well as whites accepted the one-drop rule by 1920. In 1920 the last census count was taken of mulattoes—thereafter there was not even that merely formal legal recognition of individuals of mixed black and white race.[33]

When the state governments reorganized after Reconstruction, the former slave states, with the sole exception of West Virginia, passed stringent laws against interracial marriage. Virginia continued to define a Negro as anyone with a black grandparent until 1910, when the definition was changed to "one-sixteenth" or a great-great-grandparent. By 1930 the Virginia legislature deferred to public opinion and defined a Negro as anyone with any Negro ancestry at all.[34] Most of the southern and western states defined a Negro as anyone with at least a Negro great-grandparent, but this "one-eighth" rule was more liberal than public opinion all over the country.[35]

Between Reconstruction and the turn of the century, the possibility of blacks passing for whites became an obsessive phobia on the part of white southerners and a "temptation" to many whites with black ancestry. (The logic of successful passing has always precluded accurate statistics, so exposition of the various speculations is omitted here.)[36] In fact, the one-drop social reality made anyone a Negro as soon as a white person became aware of the presence of a Negro ancestor. Booker T. Washington stated this social reality in 1900: "It is a fact that, if a person is known to have one percent of African blood in his veins, he ceases to be a white man. The ninety-nine percent of Caucasian blood does not weigh by the side of the one percent of African blood. The white blood counts for nothing. The person is a Negro every time.[37]

The foregoing outline of the legal status of individuals of mixed race suggests that the American laws against miscegenation were always attempts to put widespread public attitudes and behavior into some kind of rational language. The laws varied as local mores varied over time and place. This means that American law has permitted itself a flexibility about miscegenation that could not have been possible if there were a strong tradition in the American legal community of basic human rights for all individuals.

The absence of fundamental egalitarianism is no surprise to anyone who has studied an emancipatory tradition in Feminism or Black Studies. But what is perhaps more alarming than usual about miscegenation as a legal subject is the whiplash effect—those abrupt changes in the status of individuals of mixed race from colonial times until after Reconstruction, from lower South to upper South and from upper South to the country at large. There is no consistent trend except for a move toward the total denial of the existence of individuals of mixed race. What it all amounts to is that between 1619 and 1920, the biracial system of black and white race, where "black" meant socially non-white, was reified in American racial concepts and annealed by American law.

When there were fractional definitions of who was a Negro in promulgated laws, it was usually for the purpose of regulating which couples could marry.[38] But even with these laws in place, in attitude and custom American society adhered to the one-drop rule. When antimiscegenation laws were in place, all those who were considered Negroes in the mores became Negroes by law. Thus, legally, people of mixed race had the same lack of protection under American law after Emancipation as they did during slavery.

The point is not that people of mixed race had a right to be treated better than blacks, any more than whites had such a right. Rather, that the American legal system, in mirroring the American social system, came to classify all people of mixed race as black shows that the emancipation of the slaves did not change the *theoretical structure* of racial classifications. If anything, the racism in racial classifications grew more intense and *intrinsic* after Emancipation (see Chapter 3). It is disturbing to understand that the American concept of race was primarily a rationalization for black slavery, but it is alarming to realize that this same rationalization has remained in use for over a century after Emancipation. To be racially black was considered so bad that not even the virtue of being more racially white could cancel it out in an individual (or family). It could be said that not only did the law erase all "virtue" of whiteness in anyone who had the "vice" of blackness, but that by refusing to recognize the existence of the "virtue" of whiteness

THE HISTORY OF MIXED RACE

in individuals of mixed race, the law wiped out the existence of anyone who had both the "virtue" and the "vice."

Those individuals of mixed black and white race who were ostracized by white society and annihilated in white law eventually took the only constructive action they could: They accepted both the first-order reification of race and the second-order reification of themselves as black. They accepted their social and legal designations as Negroes and positively identified themselves with those Negroes whose forebears had had fewer progeny with white folk than their own forebears had. This process of identification began on the eve of the Civil War and came to fruition in arts, letters, history, rhetoric, and music during the Harlem Renaissance.

But before considering the cultural phenomenon of the Harlem Renaissance in the history of mixed race in America, it seems appropriate to consider those past American subcultures of mixed race that E. Franklin Frazier called "racial islands."

$\boxed{9}$

Marooned!

The racial islands described by E. Franklin Frazier were communities of mixed-race people who were socially marooned from the rest of American society.[1] In the 1930s, when Frazier did his fieldwork, these people had always lived in rural areas, and their geographical isolation had made them impervious to mainstream culture and allowed them to preserve their own traditions.

The etymology of the word "maroon" is more than metaphorically relevant to such racial islands. As a noun, "maroon" refers to a color, "yellowish-red in hue, of medium saturation and low brilliance." This color word derives from the French word *marron*, which means "chestnut-colored." As a written symbol, the French word *marron* is the same as the Italian word *marron*, which means "chestnut." The English verb, "maroon," meaning "to put [a person] ashore on a desert island or coast and leave him to his fate," comes from a term for a fugitive slave or "one of a class of Negroes descended from fugitive slaves in the West Indies and Guiana." In that fugitive-slave context, the word "maroon" was derived from both the French word *marron* and the Spanish word *cimarron*, which means "wild."[2] Thus there was a situation that occurred in European colonialism in which outcasts "of color" were isolated from the rest of society for reasons having to do with their status based on race.

The racial islands documented by Frazier did not uniformly have fugitive-slave origins. But the founders of these communities were black, mixed black and white, Indian, and white-intermarrying-with-color. So these founders were all refugees from the harsh

86

social conditions imposed on black and mixed-race persons due to slavery (and on Native Americans within the wider context of colonialism). As industrialization and other market changes of the twentieth century made it more difficult for all American rural communities to remain isolated and survive in self-sufficiency, the descendants of the founders reentered mainstream American society.

Frazier discusses a scattering of racial islands surviving to the Great Depression in the Midwest, the North, and the South. All of the spokespeople of these communities seemed to have a policy of not freely admitting that they had black ancestry, even though they kept themselves apart from their white neighbors. But their attitudes toward race varied regionally: In the Midwest they were neutral toward blacks; in the North they looked most favorably upon blacks; and in the South they emphasized their separation from blacks. Frazier's descriptions of these communities are interesting in their own right; the following summaries of some of his descriptions show how biased his own evaluation of mixed-race existence was.

The remnants of the mixed community near Indian Mound, Tennessee, set the tone of these racial islands as an archipelago. Frazier visited with the seven remaining elderly grandchildren of the founder of the community. He and his secretary "traveled country roads and drove over a muddy lane and through a half-dried-up creek." They went through a wooded area and came upon a large old house with a corrugated iron roof: "From the covered porch of the house a white-haired man with a great beard came to the gate to greet us. His bronze skin and granite-like features offered scarcely a suggestion of Negro ancestry. In fact, later, when he gave a well-chronicled story of the origin and history of his family, he made no mention of Negro blood."[3]

Frazier related excerpts from the account given him by this leader and his sisters:

> The oldest ancestor of whom they had any knowledge was their great-grandfather who lived in North Carolina about 1803. After first settling in Rutherford County, he moved to the present location and took up land. It was because of this fact, they presumed, "land" was added to the family name. He was married

twice—the first wife being assuredly an Indian and the second presumably of the same race. "Our color just came from the Cherokee race. We have no Negro blood in us." By his first wife he had eight children and by his second, four. He was a primitive Baptist. When he died around 1865, he left his land—about three-hundred acres—to his children.

Frazier relates how the history of this family unfolded in the lives of four generations. The founder had eight children by his first wife: Four of these married and had thirty-six children; there were fifty grandchildren and an unknown number of great-grandchildren. Frazier's "informants" led him to a family who lived on their own farm five miles away from the original settlement. This family was the last link to the original settlement and to those who had already left, and Frazier described them approvingly:

> Their comfortable and well-furnished house was characteristic of the thrift, intelligence, and stability for which this group of mixed-bloods are noted. The father, who was the responsible head of the family, not only worked on his farm but supervised the work of white farm laborers. Although neither father nor mother had completed high school, they took a daily paper and one or two magazines and had plans for their children to get a college education.

Frazier notes that, in the early days of the settlement, there had been a rift with the local white church on account of a remark made by the minister about "dark people attending the church." But there was also a reluctance to marry Negroes on the part of the older generations within the community. When descendants left the original Indian Mound settlement, they moved to rural parts of Ohio and Illinois and to cities in Tennessee. They valued hard work, religion, pride in family, and the fact that "no member had ever been arrested or had otherwise brought disgrace upon the family name." But the extended family did not keep in contact through correspondence, and the last family reunion, held in 1917, was attended by only the descendants living in Tennessee.

One member of the Indian Mound clan, who had migrated to Ohio, married into a community of mixed-race people in Darke County, Ohio. This Ohio settlement had been founded by free people of Indian, white, and Negro forebears from North Carolina. Frazier cites an eighty-two-year-old Darke County man with blue eyes, blond hair, and pinkish skin, on the subject of his grandfather's race: "Well, there was lot of blood in our relation—Indian, Scotch-Irish, Dutch, and a little bit nigger. Grandmother could talk Dutch just as fast as she could talk. My grandfather was as white and whiter as I was. Their mixture, they got in the South before they come here."

Although this community had been a station on the Underground Railroad, its members did not marry any escaped black slaves. Some members of the Darke County settlement were known to have "passed into the white world" and others became known as distinguished Negroes. When Frazier visited this community, he noted that all sixty families owned land, lived in comfortable rural homes, and valued education and religion. In the community were a Methodist bishop, a diplomatic representative to Liberia, and a successful realtor who helped Negroes buy homes.

In the Ramapo Hills thirty miles north of New York City, there is a mixed-race community called "Jackson Whites." Frazier's "informant" was a forty-year-old woman who had graduated from Howard University, married, and returned to this community to live, in the 1920s. She explained that one hundred years earlier the community had been founded by four Boers who all had the first name John: John De Groot, John Von Doonk, John De Vries, and John Mann. Tuscarora and Delaware Indians joined them, as well as slaves owned by a nearby family in Suffern, New York. A slave called Jackson was the first Negro to marry into the community, and it was from him that the name "Jackson Whites" derived. The community was divided between a white strain and a Negro strain. In the words of Frazier's informant, "There are in this section two distinct types of 'Jackson Whites'—one set of the white variety, living on the other side of Suffern, exhibit a great lack of intelligence as compared with their fellows of the predominating Indian and colored types."

The non-white strain had the advantage of a "Jim Crow" school and some finished college, with one person receiving his Ph.D. When more blacks came into the community during the late

1920s, a sense of black racial pride and identification with Negro culture developed.

The Jackson Whites seem to be the most enduring of all the racial islands described by Frazier. Perhaps this is because new people came to join them in the twentieth century, as opposed to the one-way movement out that seems to have been typical on the other *islands*. (I first heard about the Jackson Whites, anecdotally, in the late 1960s.)

The most prominent community of mixed race in the North was the Gouldtown settlement near Bridgeton, New Jersey. Elizabeth Adams was the granddaughter of John Fenwick, who had been given a tract of land from Lord Berkeley in 1675. She left her family to form "a connection with a Negro man whose name was Gould." She was duly denounced and disinherited by her relatives but did not repent. By 1910 there were 213 living descendants of Benjamin Gould I, the great-grandson of Elizabeth Adams.

The first Goulds were joined by the Pierces, two West Indian mulatto brothers, who married Dutch women; by the Cuff family, named after a slave called "Cuff" who married his deceased owner's widow; and by the Murrays, who were of Native American ancestry. There was impressive achievement over ensuing generations, as related by the descendant cited by Frazier:

> Several of the earlier Goulds and Pierces as well as Murrays intermarried with whites, and members of their immediate offspring went away and lost their identity, they and their descendants becoming white; there have come many who have reached distinction, and in whom their native County shows merited pride, as for instance a Methodist bishop, a chaplain in the United States Army, a physician, a lawyer, a distinguished dentist, teachers, writers, journalists; and in the industrial arts, carpenters, masons, blacksmiths, wheel-wrights, painters, carriage builders, woolen spinners, and weavers; brickmakers, machinists, engineers, electricians, printers, factory men, sailors, ministers of the Gospel, and farmers; in fact none of its sister villages has produced—taking equality of environment—more or better or more creditable individualites than has this settlement.

However, despite these distinctions, which Frazier called a "leavening element in the Negro population," the settlement was dying out when Frazier wrote about it, and the family reunions had been reduced to "an annual Sunday-School picnic, which gathers on the third Thursday in August."

The racial islands in the South did not do as well. In Columbus County, North Carolina, a settlement was begun by a man who was white, Indian, and Negro. His family intermarried with a mixed black and white family. The resulting Croatan group intermarried with the Croatan Indians in nearby Robeson County, although those Indians disassociated themselves from the connection with the mulatto settlement. This disassociation was partly caused by white politicians who wanted to disenfranchise Negroes: They secured the support of the Indians with promises of educational and social advancement, on the condition that the Croatan Indians repudiate the Negroes. Eventually the mixed-race Columbus County settlement accepted Negro designation. Only the old-timers took pride in their mixed-race ancestry, as expressed by one old woman:

> The tribe is all mixed up now more than they used to be. During the old times we had a separate feeling. We did not belong to the Negro or the whites. That's what started them to marrying first cousins. They were just freed about two miles from here. I guess you know how people just freed feel toward people of this settlement who had been free all the time. We was what was considered the "Old Free Issue," and those just freed was the "New Free Issue." They did not have much [racial] mixture. They did not like us and we did not like them. They felt that they could not accept their inferiority.

Finally, Frazier describes an impoverished community of Baptist Cajuns in Mobile County, Alabama. Although the children insisted that they were "Injuns an' white folks, all mixed up" and that they "ain't had no nigger blood in them," they lived in more backward conditions than Negro children on the plantations. Frazier quotes Horace Mann Bond here:

> In these Cajun communities where the families are brought in open contact with the white world the demoralization seems to

be even more thorough. The Creoles simply disappear, while echoes of the Cajuns linger on in tales of licentious conduct, concubinage with both white and black men, and altogether a lingering survival of the disorganization now patent in the community, but even more raw and unpleasant when exposed to the probing forces from two sides.

Frazier did not seem to regret the obliteration of the category of mixed race, which the decline of the racial islands he approved of symbolized. Rather, what Frazier valued in those communities was their patriarchal family structure, which brought what he saw as the enlightenment of white civilization to what was ultimately to be Negro culture. In summing up his discussion of the racial islands, he made his endorsement of patriarchy crystal clear:

> What, then, have been the contributions of those families of mixed blood that have fused with the Negro to the development of Negro family life? First among these contributions was their part in strengthening patriarchal traditions. In all these hybrid communities where it has been possible to trace family traditions, male progenitors were reported as the founders of the family lines.[4]

But by Frazier's own accounts, it is not true that the founders of documented lines were always male progenitors. The most prosperous and best documented of all the racial islands was the Gouldtown settlement founded by Elizabeth Adams, or at least by Elizabeth Adams *and* the black man she left her white heritage for. Furthermore, one of the family's own historians wrote "Gould's tradition a hundred years ago was 'We descended from Lord Fenwick.'"[5] Lord Fenwick was Elizabeth Adams's grandfather. Frazier also discusses the "so-called Moors of Delaware," a respectable clan, documented by the attorney general of that state, that was founded by a couple consisting of a mysterious white woman called "Regua" and a slave from the Congo River, whom she had purchased directly off a slave-trading vessel.[6]

Although Frazier thought that patriarchal family structures were more important than mixed-race family identities, he was not against racial miscegenation. Rather, he thought that amalgamation would raise the level of black culture through a strengthening of black patriarchy.[7] That is, for Frazier, racial mixing was desirable because it was a vehicle for the acculturation that he thought was desirable: "Although the peculiar cultural traits of these mixed families have been modified as they have increasingly mingled with the general Negro population, nevertheless, they have tended to enrich the family traditions of the Negro and give stability to his family life."[8]

Frazier's dismissal of the category of mixed race as something that might be valuable in itself, as he held the category of Negro race to be, places him as an intellectual product of the Harlem Renaissance. But Frazier was looking toward acculturation as a continuing hope for the future. The leaders of the Harlem Renaissance saw the white acculturation of people of mixed race, which had already been accomplished, as a way to repair some of the damage done to black people in the past: White culture could be amalgamated with black culture to "help" it. But whereas the Harlem Renaissance glorified the African origins of black culture, Frazier was more interested in the redemptive values of white civilization—his attitude toward mixed race was that it served a missionary-type function. Had Frazier been white, his patriarchal and European biases would have been understandable; but he was black—of mixed race—and in that context, his attitude is incomprehensible unless one reads his focus on patriarchy as somehow a-racial.

To return to the history of mixed race in the broader sense, those peoples who were marooned on racial islands in the United States eventually returned to the larger society one by one or in small numbers, but always on the terms of the larger society. And those terms were the one-drop rule: They either had to deny their non-white ancestry and pass for white or deny their white ancestry and *pass for black*. Frazier's informants showed an immensely subtle understanding of the one-drop rule when they made it clear that they kept to themselves and in the same breath denied black ancestry. They must have realized that the very admission of black ancestry would undermine a non-black racial identity of any sort, as far as outsiders were concerned. And they must have had fixed traditions in how they recounted their histories to their children, so that the children would learn how to dissimulate to outsiders at the same time that they learned the truth about their ancestry.

Frazier does not speculate about the confusions of personal identity or the soul searching that must have been occasioned when those who left racial islands made their either–or choices. Surely the reentry would have been exciting and adventuresome to young adults leaving declining rural settlements; but the price paid in alienation and loss of connections with the past through family history must have been dear. One can imagine an initial enthusiasm slowly dissolving into the bleak regret that what had been passed on to them could not be given to their children. To be born on an island, where one grew up a whole person, and then to find oneself marooned on the mainland and missing a vital part of that whole person! Why *couldn't* Frazier have any sympathy for that particular tragedy? The answer to this question can be found in the literature and scholarship of the Harlem Renaissance.

10

The Harlem Renaissance: Cultural Suicide

The one-drop rule excluded everyone with a known black ancestor from white society, and the antimiscegenation laws criminalized mixed-race marriages and illegitimized the children of mixed-race unions. Nevertheless, according to the 1910 census, 21 percent of the black population was of visible mixed race.[1] As Joel Williamson points out, a distinction should be made between these visibly mixed-race mulattoes and the 75 percent of the designated black population that the same 1910 census calculated as having genetic white ancestry. Both the 21 percent and the 75 percent (which included the visible 21 percent) belonged to the generic group of mulattoes, but only the 21 percent looked to be of mixed race (or looked white, in some cases).[2] Intersecting the visibly mixed-race blacks and the presumably pure-race blacks was the class of successful blacks that W.E.B. Du Bois called the "Talented Tenth."[3] This talented tenth was in large part, although not entirely, composed of a *mulatto elite*. The mulatto elite was mostly made up of visibly mixed-race blacks, including blacks who looked completely white (some of them may have been completely white genetically, because there is no way to know whether they had any of the genes of their known black ancestors, three or more generations back in their family histories). In 1918, Edward Reuter reported that out of 4,267 blacks who had "made any marked success in life, 3,820 were mulattoes."[4]

The mulatto elite was excluded from white society and both admired and resented by less economically and culturally advantaged blacks. This elite had generations of higher education, economic security, and social refinement in its families by 1910. The members of this caste had the best chance of passing for white—they knew more about white culture than the mass of blacks and had more contact with whites. It was traditional for the mulatto elite to keep itself aloof from the mass of blacks: Many were proud of long family histories of freedom that predated the Civil War; many descended from illustrious white ancestors.[5] However, the Harlem Renaissance marked an abrupt change in this entire tradition of exclusivity within black culture.

During the Harlem Renaissance of the 1920s, the talented tenth, which was in large part made up of the mulatto elite, took up the task of defining and describing American blacks, to American blacks. It has been said that during the Harlem Renaissance, black Americans became aware of themselves as a people and that they united as a people.[6] It has also been objected that American blacks were by the 1920s too diverse within themselves to be a people or for such a union to be possible.[7] But both the belief in union and the denial of its having taken place usually fail to make a clear reference to the boundaries within which black Americans did or could unite. They did or could unite within the boundaries of their race, as their race was defined by white Americans. As defined by white Americans, the black race included people who were completely racially black, people who were mostly racially black, people who were one-half racially white, people who were mostly racially white, and people who were completely racially white according to any physical measurement of race available but who had at least one known black ancestor. The visibly mixed-race blacks and visibly white-race blacks threw in their lot with the apparently pure-race blacks.[8] Publicly, the talented tenth assumed positions of cultural leadership within the new (to them) combined black group, which was, of course, the old and only black group from the standpoint of white America. Socially, the mulatto elite officially removed their old barriers against marrying darker-skinned blacks; they retained these barriers only as matters of personal preference, snobbery, and what was later to be called self-hate, inauthenticity, and color-struck(ness) from black points of view.[9]

During the Harlem Renaissance, the people who were designated non-white in the sense of black, by white America, all took up their black designation on the premise of a democracy among themselves. This was a magnificent enterprise: Much was gained in black pride, culture, and achievement, and nothing of *substance*, of immediate practical value, was lost. What was lost was the concept of mixed race as a theoretical wedge against racism and against the concept of physical race—the new combined black community threw away any effective intellectual weapon against American racial designations, which is to say, against the core of American racism. It lost all means of challenging the asymmetrical kinship schema of racial inheritance and the attendant oppressive biracial system. Designated American blackness, as a cultural force capable of defeating American racism, thereby cut off its own head during the Harlem Renaissance.

This theoretical-wedge aspect of mixed race probably accounts for the vilification of miscegenation and people of mixed race by racists of all races. If it is possible for people to be of mixed race, based on their genetic endowment alone, then *race* is not an essential or even an important division between human beings, either naturally or culturally. If race were a natural division, individuals of mixed race would simply not exist. If race were something cultural, then the person of mixed race, in learning, working, and otherwise functioning socially in both racial cultures—especially the dominant racial culture—would overcome cultural barriers. Furthermore, if individuals of mixed race are granted a separate racial identity, then all of the myths of racial purity and stability break down because there is then such a large universe of possible races that the historical contingency of any group's racial identity becomes transparent.

But everyone in the great mass of all Americans in the 1920s had sound reasons to overlook the theoretical loss in the emancipatory tradition: The mass of blacks needed leadership and cultural pride. The whites were more obsessed than ever with their own racial purity, exclusivity, and superiority, delusions that were all reinforced by the cultural celebration of, by, and for those people whom they designated black—to the extent that whites were aware of the Harlem Renaissance.[10] And the mulatto elite and those of visible racial mixture, in general, needed a broader identity than their own narrow class could provide. Because they were barred from white society, the mulatto elite needed productive avenues for expression. Also, people of visible mixed race were devalued by both blacks and whites, and the broader cultural identity of all blacks brought the protection of a much larger group than a mere 21 percent of what was already a minority of 10 percent.[11]

Many blacks left their rural communities of origin in the South from 1914 to 1930, due to an economic depression, the ravages of the cotton boll weevil, and massive flooding. Most of these blacks moved to other southern areas, but many came to northern cities. By 1930 the black population in New York City had increased 250 percent to 327,706, and almost all blacks lived in Harlem.[12] At that time James Weldon Johnson described Harlem as "a black city located in the heart of white Manhattan . . . a miracle straight out of the skies." But this mecca was also a segregated slum: Thirty percent of all dwellings lacked bathing facilities; the death rate from tuberculosis was five times greater than for whites in Manhattan; schools were segregated and education for blacks reflected their predominant employment in domestic service and unskilled labor and their exclusion from skilled blue-collar, clerical, and professional work.

During this period, political and civil conditions were also dire for blacks. From 1896 to 1904, the U.S. Supreme Court upheld southern strategies to deprive blacks of their voting rights; the court also upheld southern laws that segregated all public facilities, including schools and housing. In the North, theaters, restaurants, hotels, housing, and schools were also segregated, even where the law forbade it.

President Theodore Roosevelt first praised black troops for their valor during the Battle of San Juan Hill, then called them cowards while he publicly praised former Confederate leaders. Roosevelt also expressed approval of the lynching of blacks on the basis of the widely held myth that white female sexual purity was endangered by black male sexual bestiality. President William Howard Taft endorsed restrictions on black suffrage and began the segregation of federal offices in Washington, D.C., a policy that was expanded during President Woodrow Wilson's administration. President Warren G. Harding denounced racial amalgamation. Most American blacks were patriotic during World War I, but in the segregated military black troops did not receive the same support services as did white troops.

The recorded lynchings of blacks by white mobs declined from 150 a year in the 1890s to 75 a year after 1905. But in 1900 race riots in southern cities, as well as in New York and Springfield, Illinois, resulted in indiscriminate black deaths and property destruction by white mobs. Race riots and lynchings continued through the First World War. In 1918 a Tennessee newspaper advertised the burning of a "live negro," and the event drew three-thousand spectators! In 1919, after the war, a new wave of race riots swept twenty cities, to the indifference or encouragement of local police. But by this time many blacks had armed themselves and were firing back on white mobs.

That American blacks could begin a self-aware cultural movement against this background of terror is impressive by any world historical standards. Therefore, it should be kept in mind that any criticism of the Harlem Renaissance rejection of the category of mixed race as a neutral category between black and white races is *theoretical*; this theoretical criticism is relevant only to choices available later in history. At the time of the Harlem Renaissance, white society did not publicly profess racial neutrality as one of its ideals, as it does today (hypocritically or not). At the time of the Harlem Renaissance, white society was openly anti-black, and the one-drop rule was not a neutral theoretical demarcation but an expression and reinforcement of the low esteem in which whites held blacks. Langston Hughes made this clear through his character Simple:

> "Black is powerful. You can have ninety-nine drops of white blood in your veins down South—but if that other *one* drop is black, shame on you! Even if you look white, you're black. That drop is really powerful. Explain it to me. You're colleged."
>
> "It has no basis in science," I said, "so there's no logical explanation."[13]

In 1916, Madison Grant, a graduate of Columbia and Yale universities, who was a lawyer in New York with an avocation in Zoology, wrote *The Passing of the Great Race*. Drawing on Darwinism, Grant argued that whites had physically evolved to such a specialized level of mental, moral, and social organization that they were vulnerable to mixture with "lower" races. According to Grant, the result of white and non-white racial mixing would always be a race reverting to the "lower race" in evolutionary specialization. Therefore, Grant reasoned, the mix of a white man and an Indian was an Indian; a white man and a Negro, a Negro; a white man and a Hindu, a Hindu; and any European race and a Jew, a Jew.

It wasn't until World War II that social scientists developed the consensus that racial mixing simply resulted in intermediate types (in those contexts in which they still spoke of races).[14] In the 1920s, the only approved and legal form of racial mixing was within the designated black race, and even this was a liberalization of earlier laws in some states that had barred marriage between blacks and mulattoes.[15]

This *intra*-racial mixing between 'mulattoes' (where 'malatto' refers to any degree of visible white ancestry) and blacks probably accelerated in the decades following the Civil War, when the end of slavery not only resulted in greater segregation between blacks and whites but in a decline of black female concubinage by white males.[16] By the 1900s, the entire Negro population was becoming more brown in appearance, and by the 1940s students of physical race estimated that only 10 percent of the Negro population was racially pure black.[17] The old mulatto elite, which had been culturally advantaged for many generations as well as socially privileged due to light skin color, would be supplanted by a Negro elite in the decades following World War II.[18] This Negro elite would construct an ideology of ideals of blackness in increasingly symbolic meanings of "black," as a word in any way related to skin color (not unlike the word "white").

It is a paradox that the leaders of the Harlem Renaissance, in turning to Negro experience for the content of Negro culture, combined their own white European cultural traditions with pan-Africanism, a new appreciation of southern Negro rural life, the human dignity of Negro slaves, and early twentieth-century Negro urban poverty.[19] This combination was both a focus on the distinctive present joys and vitality in Negro art, music, and social relations and a direct engagement with the question of what it meant to be a Negro in America, that is, the question of Negro identity.[20] The paradox rests on the mixed-race ancestry of Harlem Renaissance leaders such as W.E.B. Du Bois, Jean Toomer, Countee Cullen, Langston Hughes, Zora Neale Hurston, and James Weldon Johnson.[21] It was as if these writers, in combining white with black, culturally, within a black racial framework, *acted out* their own mixed-race ancestry without daring to fully confront it. It was daring for many of the "aristocrats of color" to embrace mass black culture. That they did not insist on their white cultural heritage with equal force may have been both prudence in the face of discrimination and a defiance and repudiation of their whiteness.

It is unremarkable that the late nineteenth-century accommodationist Negro leaders, personified by Booker T. Washington, would not attach any racial significance to themselves on account of white forebears. (Washington simply said that his father was said to have been white and never took an interest in him; he also praised the high moral character of the woman who was to become his second wife for her declining an opportunity to pass for white.)[22] But it is remarkable that when it came to their own family histories, Du Bois and the other Harlem Renaissance spokespeople simply passed over the issue of miscegenation insofar as it might have placed them in a distinct racial category. At a time when the whole black race was becoming visibly brown and when brown was even an ideal, it could not have been a reluctance to offend darker-skinned Negroes that caused this omission. Many of the Harlem Renaissance leaders were a breath away from redefining both themselves and the majority of Negroes as neither black nor white or as both, but they did not do so. The closest these New Negro spokespeople came to such a redefinition was a glorification of brown skin colors in poetry, song, romantic preference, and prize fighting (e.g., Joe Lewis as the "The Brown Bomber").[23] There were many moments in the work of Harlem Renaissance writers and others when it could have been said, in the words of Charles W. Chesnutt's character John Warwick, in *The House behind the Cedars*, "You must take us for ourselves alone—we are new people." Indeed, Joel Williamson places this quotation at the beginning of his book *New People*.

Williamson is a careful historian on the subject of miscegenation and 'mulattoness' and his data is widely respected in the literature on mixed race. But Williamson's new people were new people within black America only and not new people between, alongside, or even outside of black *and* white America. When Williamson interprets the Harlem Renaissance as a "marriage" between black and white culture, it is exclusively a marriage within black culture. And when he speaks of the literal marriages between blacks and whites that resulted in the color brown, he is talking about intra-racial mixing. This is how Williamson refers to his subject:

> Confronted with the rock-hard exclusiveness of the white world, the mulatto leaders of the Renaissance turned back to the black. They changed the mission of the mulatto elite from one of carrying white culture to the Negro mass to one of picking up black culture within the Negro world and marrying it smoothly to the white culture they knew so well. . . . It meant that the young vanguard of the mulatto elite was about to dissolve itself as a vanguard based on color. It signified the essential acceptance by the Negro world of the one-drop rule, a rule that was virtually the antithesis of assimilation. Finally, and most important, it meant that Afro-Americans would begin to build a separate culture—one that was neither white nor black, but both. The result would be a new Negro culture and a new Negro people.[24]
> . . . By the 1920's a hundred years of intensive mixing between blacks and mulattoes was producing, physically, the "brown American." . . . At the same time, Negro artists and intellectuals in the Renaissance were generating a mixture of black and white culture that was equally "brown."

Williamson has even more trouble with his metaphors when he moves on to generalizations about Negro American culture at the end of the 1970s: "The people are brown and so too is the culture.

Even so, 'black' does not seem a misnomer as applied to Negro culture in America. Negro culture is indeed precisely black in that it is not white."[25]

The mixed racial metaphors are all that has been mixed on a conceptual level in Williamson's endorsement of the label "black." Neither the leaders of the Harlem Renaissance nor Williamson, writing sixty years later, could free themselves from the intellectual tyranny of the one-drop rule. They did not and perhaps could not conceptualize a category of mixed black and white race as a racial category distinct from black race, in the same way that black race has always been distinct from white race. This conceptual block was straightforwardly expressed in specific literary moments by Du Bois, Hughes, Johnson, and Hurston, and it was implied in the perceived contradiction between Toomer's work and life. Some of these literary moments are considered in the remainder of this chapter.

W.E.B. Du Bois founded *The Crisis*, the monthly publication of the National Association for the Advancement of Colored People (NAACP), in 1910, and he edited it until 1934.[26] Du Bois was the most prominent American Negro during those years.[27] He was critical of the ideal of artistic freedom in the literary dimension of the Harlem Renaissance, and he had harsh words for the realistic depictions of impoverished and disorganized (according to white standards—see Chapter 5) black life, because he thought that such representations were undermining to black racial morale, black racial self-respect, and the good opinions that he hoped whites would form about blacks.[28] Nevertheless, Du Bois helped many Harlem Renaissance writers; his preeminence as a scholar and a chronicler of black experience is generally taken for granted in the context of the Harlem Renaissance quest for black identity.[29] Du Bois is famous for his description of American black experience as a life behind a "veil" and for his statement that *the* problem of the twentieth century would be "the problem of the color line."[30]

Du Bois was always on the black side of this color line, both in physical appearance and in his claim that blacks had a dual consciousness.[31] The dual consciousness consisted in a black person's knowledge of self and of other blacks, as they were, versus a black person's experience of self and of other blacks, as whites saw them.[32] However, for Du Bois the black knowledge of white-experience-of-blacks was always an alien awareness. Du Bois did not recognize cultural whiteness as a positive aspect of black experience, as for example, Countee Cullen or Jean Toomer might have done.[33]

Du Bois's paternal great-grandfather was a French Huguenot who had two sons with a mulatto woman.[34] Du Bois's mother was of Dutch and African ancestry. He described his maternal grandmother as "yellow" and his father as a "light mulatto." He wrote of his paternal grandfather as "'colored' but quite white in appearance." That Du Bois put the word "colored" in quotes suggests that he may not have considered his grandfather colored. This, as well as the following passage, indicates that Du Bois was sharply aware of racial mixtures among his people (he is here writing about the town of Great Barrington, Massachusetts, where he grew up):

> The color line was manifest and yet not absolutely drawn. I remember a cousin of mine who brought home a white wife. The chief objection was that he was not able to support her and nobody knew about her family; and knowledge of family history was counted as highly important. Most of the colored people had some white blood from unions several generations past. That they congregated together in their own social life was natural because that was the rule in town.

As Du Bois relates his childhood through high school, he had a close relationship with his mother, and the well-principled New Englanders of Great Barrington provided him with an adequate education and appreciated his musical talent. However, when he completed high school, it became clear that there were few opportunities in Great Barrington for an educated colored person, and he was sent south to Fisk University in Tennessee. He was happy to go and described his enthusiasm while using very literal terms for his racial designation. It never occurred to him that he might be something other than or something in addition to a person of color, racially: "I started out and went into Tennessee at the age of seventeen to be a sophomore at Fisk University. It was to me an extraordinary experience. I was thrilled to be for the first time many people of my own color or rather of such various extraordinary colors, which I had only glimpsed before, b seemed were bound to me by new and exciting and eterna

Thus Du Bois was aware of the cultural determinants of racial designations. He was also aware of how racial designations appear to refer to natural facts about people. He knew that he was both black and white, according to the natural facts of his ancestry. But he did not use a mixed-race designation for himself, based either on his ancestry or on his early participation in white culture. None of this is to suggest that Du Bois was not black or is not a colossus of distinctly black cultural history. The point is that Du Bois was also white and that he was educated in the traditions of white culture. This is not merely an abstract point—he had white teachers, white friends, and white well-wishers in Great Barrington all through his childhood, up until the time he went to Fisk University. Nevertheless, despite this whiteness of ancestry and culture, Du Bois identified himself as black and expected other people to do the same. Externally he may have had no choice in how he identified himself, and his struggles for black emancipation were all within the black identification. But if one is committed to a struggle anyway, why accept as parameters of that struggle, the parameters that have been drawn by one's oppressors?

Zora Neale Hurston was in the center of Harlem's black bohemia, along with Wallace Thurman, Langston Hughes, and Rudolph Fisher.[36] As did Du Bois, Hurston grew up under circumstances that were relatively free of oppression by white people. Her home was in the black town of Eatonville, Florida, which had been incorporated under the benignity of the Civil War Union veterans who had founded the nearby city of Maitland.[37] Again parallel to Du Bois, Hurston's early studies were in the social sciences. She was a student of Franz Boas at Columbia University, and she later worked with Melville Herskovits in collecting data for his *Anthropometry of the American Negro*. But unlike Du Bois, Hurston was neither aristocratic in attitude nor conventional about morals or women.[38] Her most successful novel, *Their Eyes Were Watching God*, was about Janie, a poor, uneducated black woman in the rural South, who gains self-confidence in the course of three marriages and finally suits herself in a quest for love.[39] Alain Locke, the Howard University philosophy professor who was the good patron of many young Harlem Renaissance writers, including Hurston, wrote a bad review of this book. Hurston then denounced him as a "malicious spiteful little snot," and a hypocrite, and a plagiarist, who used his academic credentials to gain undeserved cultural power. Hurston had a lifelong reputation for being as outspoken as she wanted to be.[40]

Hurston was an avid student of black folk culture. She described the asymmetry in black art and the importance of mimicry, drama, and communality in black life from an aesthetic as well as an anthropological perspective. Hurston herself was middle-class, educated, and light in complexion.[41] (She looked like a Native American; the great love of her life, "A.W.P.," said that she reminded him "of the Indian on the Skookum Apples.")[42] But Hurston was more outspoken than Du Bois, and in her autobiography she expressed an awareness of both the pride and the shame that designated black Americans associated with white ancestry. She also explicitly referred to herself as of mixed race. The following passage eloquently covers those issues:

> I see no benefits in excusing my looks by claiming to be half Indian. In fact, I boast that I am the only Negro in the United States whose grandfather on the mother's side was *not* an Indian chief. Neither did I descend from George Washington, Thomas Jefferson, or any other Governor of a Southern state. I see no need to manufacture me a legend to beat the facts. I do not coyly admit to a touch of the tarbrush to my Indian and white ancestry. You can consider me Old Tar-Brush in person if you want to. I am a mixed blood, it is true, but I differ from the party line in that I neither consider it an honor nor a shame. I neither claim Jefferson as my grandpa, nor exclaim, "Just look how that white man took advantage of my grandma!" . . . it is a well-known fact that no matter where two sets of people come together, there are bound to be some in-betweens.[43]

However, although Hurston was more provocative than Du Bois in describing herself racially, she was exactly like Du Bois in staunchly taking up a black identity: "I maintain that I have been a Negro three time—a Negro baby, a Negro girl, and a Negro woman."[44]

Langston Hughes wrote in a voice that still has contemporary style. He brought the Harlem Renaissance to life vividly with his descriptions of its parties.[45] A'Lelia Walker was a great Harlem party-giver in the 1920s. She entertained lavishly on the fortune she had inherited from her mother, the entrepreneur of "Madame Walker's Hair Straightening Process." When A'Lelia Walker died in 1931, Hughes marked her funeral as the end of the Harlem Renaissance: "That was really the end of the gay times of the New Negro era in Harlem, the period that had begun to reach its end when the crash came in 1929 and the white people had much less money to spend on themselves, and practically none to spend on Negroes, for the depression brought everybody down a peg or two. And the Negroes had but few pegs to fall."

But after this assessment in his autobiography, *The Big Sea*, Hughes goes on to write about parties uptown:

409 Edgecombe, Harlem's tallest and most exclusive apartment house. . . . The Walter Whites and the Aaron Douglasses, among others, lived and entertained here. Walter White was a jovial and cultured host, with a sprightly mind, and an apartment overlooking the Hudson. He had the most beautiful wife in Harlem, and they were always hospitable to hungry literati like me.

At the Aaron Douglasses', although he was a painter, more young writers were found than painters. Usually everybody would chip in and go dutch on the refreshments, calling down to the nearest bootlegger for a bottle of whatever it was that was drunk in those days, when labels made no difference at all in the liquid content—Scotch, bourbon, rye, and gin being the same except for coloring matter.

There were also parties downtown:

I remember one at Florine Sterrheimer's. Another at V. F. Calverton's and another at Bob Chandler's where the walls were hung with paintings and Louise Helstrom served the drinks. Paul Haakon, who was a kid then whom Louise had "discovered" somewhere, danced and everybody Oh'ed and Ah'ed, and said what a beautiful young artist! What an artist! But later when nobody was listening, Paul Haakon said to me: "Some baloney—I'm no artist, I'm in Vaudeville."

Hughes's report of his mixed-race ancestry is almost as breezy as his chronicle of the parties:

On my father's side, the white blood in his family came from a Jewish slave trader in Kentucky, Silas Cushenberry, of Clark County, who was his mother's father; and Sam Clay, a distiller of Scotch descent, living in Henry County, who was his father's father. So on my father's side both male great-grandparents were white, and Sam Clay was said to be a relative of the great statesman, Henry Clay, his contemporary.

On my mother's side, I had a paternal great-grandfather named Quarles—Captain Ralph Quarles—who was white and who lived in Louisa County, Virginia, before the Civil War, and who had several colored children by a colored housekeeper, who was his slave. The Quarles traced their ancestry back to Francis Quarles, famous Jacobean poet, who wrote *A Feast for Wormes*.

On my maternal grandmother's side, there was French and Indian blood. My grandmother looked like an Indian—with very long black hair.[46]

Hughes's grandmother raised him with a strong pride in family. His parents separated because his father hated poor people and American "niggers" who would not leave the country that treated them badly. His father was a successful businessman in Mexico.[47]

Despite his white ancestry and his father's attitude, Langston Hughes accepted the one-drop rule and saw himself as an American Negro. When he went to Africa he called it "The Great Africa of My Dreams." There was also disappointment: "There was one thing that hurt me a lot when I talked with the people. The Africans looked at me and would not believe I was a Negro." Immediately after these words, Hughes captions a new section "NEGRO." Then he begins, "You see, unfortunately, I am not black." And after Hughes explains the American one-drop rule, he says, "I am brown."[48]

There is an interesting equivocation of values associated with Hughes's use of the word "brown." In the American context it is unfortunate for Hughes to be brown because his white ancestry is obliterated. But in the African context it is unfortunate for Hughes to be brown because his black ancestry has been diluted. As he puts it, "In Africa, the word [Negro] is more pure. It means *all* Negro, therefore *black*."

This equivocation of values in the word "brown" is not explicitly analyzed by Hughes. Instead, he presents it all in a flash, in the text quoted above.

The literary moment in which Hughes chooses blackness unequivocally is implicit. But the implication in his text is all the more definitive of his identity because he is throughout so embedded in black culture. Hughes describes the surfaces of black culture so smoothly that there is no way the reader can raise a question of mixed race to Hughes, the writer, without violating the unspoken rules of politeness in his rhetorical space. It is an exquisite and elaborate kind of politeness that is at stake here, the kind of politeness that allows people to enjoy their lives with grace, under pressures that are totally lacking in grace. Hughes's rhetorical rules are very like the unspoken rules for acceptable behavior at a party!

Nathan Eugene "Jean" Toomer was, to use Williamson's phrase, "lighter in culture" than DuBois, Hurston, and Hughes. His grandfather P.B.S. Pinchback was the son of a rich Virginia planter and his slave, whom he freed. "Pink" Pinchback was educated in Ohio, spent an adventurous youth on the riverboats, married a light-skinned black Memphis belle, and served as a captain in the Union army during the Civil War. For forty days during Reconstruction he was the acting governor of Louisiana. His daughter married a light mulatto named Toomer who deserted her when their son Jean was born. Jean Toomer was raised by his grandparents in Washington, D.C., among the mulatto elite who were called "The Four Hundred" at the turn of the twentieth century.[49]

Toomer was handsome, brilliant, and vain, and he never really settled down. After his grandparents died, he took a teaching job in rural Georgia. His poetic novel, *Cane*, published in 1923, was the result of this experience in the South. *Cane* is Toomer's only major work and perhaps the greatest work of art to come out of the Harlem Renaissance. It is a series of vignettes about the love lives and sensibilities of poor rural blacks, with a middle section about the psychological pain of the mulatto elite among whites. The work seamlessly combines poetry and prose throughout, as the following vignette exemplifies:

NIGHT

(Foxie, the bitch, slicks back her ears and barks at the rising moon.)
Wind is in the corn. Come along.
Corn leaves swaying, rusty with talk,
Scratching choruses above the guinea's squawk.
Wind is in the corn. Come along.

Carma's tale is the crudest melodrama. Her husband's in the gang. And it's her fault he got there. Working with a contractor, he was away most of the time. She had others. No one blames her for that. He returned one day and hung around the town where he picked up week-old boasts and rumors. . . . Bane accused her. She denied. He couldn't see that she was becoming hysterical. He would have liked to take his fists and beat her. Who was strong as a man. Stronger. Words, like corkscrews, wormed to her strength. It fizzled out. Grabbing a gun, she rushed from the house and plunged across the road into a cane-break. . . . There in quarter heaven shone the crescent moon. . . . Bane was afraid to follow till he heard the gun go off.[50]

The great irony about Toomer is that even though *Cane* was a premier contribution to black culture, Toomer himself was not securely black in his identity. Williamson says that he "ricocheted" between blackness and whiteness like William Faulkner's character Joe Christmas.[51] Langston Hughes made fun of Toomer's association with the Russian mystic George Gurdjieff and snidely implied that Toomer left Harlem and married a white novelist for money.[52] At a time when Toomer was distancing himself from his blackness and from black literature, he accused Alain Locke of reprinting selections from *Cane* without his permission.[53] Toomer would not allow his poems to appear in James Weldon Johnson's

Book of American Negro Poetry, on the grounds that he was "no more colored than white."[54]

The irony of Toomer's defection from black society suggests that his own aesthetic experience as expressed in *Cane* was not the final form of the way in which he experienced life. If this is correct, this makes Toomer an ironist in Richard Rorty's sense of an artist who never does have a "final language."[55] This is not the place to interpret Gurdjieff, but it is also significant that Gurdjieff's main premise was that human beings are not born with souls but can create their own souls by living according to prescribed disciplines.[56] So if Toomer defected from blackness, it could not have been an easy passing into a conventional white world. Rather, something in the nature of transcendence of racial concepts, racism, and conventional human society is implied. But as valuable as such transcendence is, Toomer's transcendence did not directly address the issue of mixed race in the context in which it was presented to him; he took the category up for himself, privately, but not in a dialogue with those mundane forces that oppressed him. And it may be that the very privateness of his resolution of his racial identity made the combination of his life and his work something of an embarrassment to the black cultural tradition. One wonders if Toomer would have found it necessary to say he was "no more colored than white" had he not been well known as the writer of *Cane*. But if he had simply claimed whiteness, it would have been another form of the cultural suicide of mixed race, a mere mirror image of the black racial identities chosen by Du Bois, Hurston, and Hughes.

11

Genocidal Images of Mixed Race

n American history, racism as a form of oppression was first instigated by whites against blacks. The acts of kidnapping, theft, rape, mutilation, and murder that were committed by whites against blacks since the beginning of slavery were accompanied by images "in" white minds of blacks as criminal and uncivilized. As John Langston Gwaltney points out, blacks also had images of whites as criminal and uncivilized (see Chapter 4). But whereas the white images could be called "projection" in a technical psychological sense, the black images seem to be direct representations of oppression. Still, the white images of blacks have always been more powerful than the black images of whites—whites are scarcely aware of the black images of whites, and blacks are all too aware of the white images of blacks. However, both black and white images of people of mixed race have been so destructive to mixed-race identity that it is still unthinkable to blacks and whites that mixed-race people might have distinct images of blacks, whites, or even themselves.

In the *Devil's Dictionary*, compiled between 1881 and 1906, this is how Ambrose Bierce defined a person of mixed race: "MULATTO, *n.* A child of two races, ashamed of both."[1] Bierce's lexicography was deliberately cynical, and his other racial entries would be considered racist today.[2] But one does not have to be cynical or racist to understand how shame could motivate white images of mulattoes: The existence of mulattoes is the result of violations of sexual taboos upheld by white people, and in American history the violations were traditionally initiated by white men.

The shame of the mulatto, albeit unjustified, is complex, depending on how the mulatto views himself. From the standpoint of mixed race, the mulatto does not fit into the American biracial system. This difference in itself can cause many types of negative self-valuation. If the mulatto sees herself as black, she may feel shame because her existence could have been occasioned by the result of harm done to a black ancestress by a white person.[3] If the mulatto sees herself as white, which she can do only by denying the existence of black forebears, then her black forebears may be an occasion for shame, not only because they have to be denied but because of the devaluation of blacks by whites. But American mulattoes have rarely had the luxury of a racial identity different from that of whites or blacks. They have therefore had no ground on which to be ashamed of both races. So, ironically, Bierce's quip presents a rosy picture of mulatto consciousness, and it has no foundation in American social reality.

People ought to feel ashamed only for what they have done. That one is given or denied a certain racial designation cannot in any rational, or reasonable, or humanly decent sense be a cause for shame. Mulattoes therefore have no reason to feel ashamed of whites, blacks, or themselves on the ground of their mulattoness. However, both whites and blacks have created and retained images of mulattoes that should have made them ashamed of themselves—mulattoes have been degraded in imagery that is genocidal to the category of mixed race. If Americans must categorize everyone into races, then they ought not to do so with annihilatory intent toward any race, including that "impure" race to which Americans of mixed black and white race presumably belong (if any races exist).

The worst white images of mulattoes came from nineteenth-century scientific speculation, which was often more bizarre than the lay devaluation of mulattoes due to the authoritative, formal style of scientific language. The worst black images of mulattoes came from black experience, which had been shaped by white racism. The best images of mulattoes came from both whites and blacks who accepted the categorization of people of mixed race as black, which is to say, who did not accept a category of mixed race.

As was discussed in Chapter 10, the theoretical relinquishment of the concept of mixed race was a key component of the identity of the New Negro, accepted by the majority of the mulatto elite during the Harlem Renaissance. Du Bois designated some mixed-race individuals as the "Talented Tenth" of all blacks.[4] And Joel Williamson, in describing the paradigm shift to the New Negro within designated black culture, says that it was necessary for the old light-skinned mulatto aristocracy literally to die out before this change could be completed.[5]

During slavery, the free mulatto elite was separate from the mass of black Americans. Many of these mulattoes were proud of their white ancestors, and they resented white images of them as no different from the mass of American blacks. Just prior to the Civil War, at the height of abolitionism, they lost many of their prerogatives in the South and began to be pressured toward broad alliances with other blacks. During Reconstruction, they accepted positions of leadership among blacks: For example, eighteen out of the twenty-two Negroes elected to the U.S. Congress from the South between 1870 and 1901 were of mixed race, although, of course, they were officially designated as black.[6]

Booker T. Washington, a mulatto, reached the peak of his popularity after his 1884 Atlanta Exposition Address. He said then that blacks and whites could be as separate and united as the "fingers on a hand," and he was endorsed by many southern whites as a responsible leader of blacks.[7] Even the most racist of American whites during this era tended to believe that designated blacks with white forebears were more intelligent, competent, and likely to succeed than racially pure blacks, on account of their white ancestry.[8] So once they were considered to be blacks, individuals of mixed black and white race were well regarded by both blacks and whites—blacks made them their leaders, and whites accepted them as black leaders. The devaluation of people of mixed black and white race occurred in contexts in which they were regarded simply as individuals of mixed race, in that mental time and space (so to speak) before they were relegated to the black race.

Americans came closest to acknowledging something more

than a biracial system of blackness and whiteness in antebellum South Carolina and Louisiana. In the 1830s, Judge William Harper of South Carolina refused to rule on the race of a man in fractional terms. He argued that while all slaves were black, outside of slavery an individual's community standing and character had to be considered in addition to black ancestry in order to designate that individual as black.[9] At the 1898 Constitutional Convention in South Carolina, George Tillman of Edgefield County proposed that the liberal standard of one black grandparent be the determinant of blackness. Otherwise, Tillman argued, many people in his community who owned property and had been loyal soldiers in the Civil War would be racially proscribed.[10]

In antebellum New Orleans, the institution of *plaçage* legitimized the support and concubinage by rich white planters of women with black ancestry. Before they were *placed*, these New Orleans Quadroons—this was the generic term, although many were octoroons and of lesser "degrees" of blackness—were displayed at fancy balls to prospective "protectors." Their mothers and other female chaperones supervised these balls, which their brothers and other male relatives were not allowed to attend. The sons and brothers of the New Orlean Quadroons were either set up in business among the respectable *gens de couleur* in the city or sent to France, where they could study or reside without stigma due to race.

It could be said that the defendant referred to by Harper and the mixed-race citizens of Edgefield County were merely tolerated, as were the free *gens de couleur*. But the New Orleans Quadroons were positively valued. Their beauty and culture were legendary, and their liaisons with upper-class whites were held in higher regard than common concubinage and considered comparable to marriage in social and legal status.[11]

In 1908, Alfred Holt Stone suggested that all people of mixed race be recognized as a separate caste, but his motives did not come from a belief, no matter how exploitative, that there was anything of positive value about mulattoes. Rather, Stone thought that because mulattoes were the natural leaders of all blacks, if they were removed from the black race and accorded separate status, they would be less likely to disrupt white society by pressing for racial equality.[2] In general, between the Civil War and World War II miscegenation was held by white society to be a great biological, cultural, and religious evil. There were two parts to this antipathy: an abhorrence of the idea and fact of interracial sex; and a strong devaluation of individuals of mixed race physically, mentally, and morally.

The scientific and popular attitudes against interracial sex ranged over a *tectonic* of interlocking beliefs: that whites were, or ought to be, revolted by sex with blacks; that it was sinful for white men to have sex with black women; that it was depraved for white women to have sex with black men; that black women deliberately set out to seduce white men; that black men obsessively lusted after white women; that it was a sin to condone miscegenation; that miscegenation was unpatriotic because it was a danger to the continuance of all that was fine in American culture. All of these beliefs were accompanied by strong feelings, and their formal expression by scientists, pseudo-scientists, and politicians wove in and out of popular and academic discussion. John G. Mencke has presented a careful summary of this ideology, although his summary is not divided into the beliefs listed above. But Mencke's citations provide examples of all of these beliefs, and the following excerpts from his citations are typical of each of the beliefs conceptualized above.

That Whites Were or Ought to Be Revolted by Sex with Blacks

In 1884, Walter B. Hill, chancellor of the University of Georgia, spoke of a "natural barrier" against amalgamation, as a racial instinct in the southern mind.[13] A year later W. C. Benet wrote in the Augusta *Chronicle*, "The proud race whose blood flows in our veins will never stoop to marriage with the negro, nor with any colored race. . . . Race fusion is so abhorrent to our race instincts and so out of accord with the history of our race that we can smile at the absurd suggestion. . . . There may be isolated cases of intermarriage, but they will never betoken a movement."[14]

That It Was Sinful for White Men to Have
Sex with Black Women

John H. Van Evrie of New York was a white supremacist, as well as a physician and an editor. In 1868 he codified many of the nineteenth-century tenets of racism against blacks, such as:

> Mulattoism is to the South what prostitution is to the North—that is, those depraved persons who give themselves up to a wicked perversion of the sexual instincts, resort to the mongrel or "colored women" instead of houses of ill-fame, as in the former case. Such a thing as love, or natural affection, never has nor can attract persons of different races, and therefore all the co-habitations of white men and negro women are abnormal—a perversion of the instincts of reproduction.[15]

That It Was Depraved for White Women to Have
Sex with Black Men

In 1915, Robert W. Shyfeld, a physician and major in the Army Medical Corps, wrote that although both Negro men and women had strong carnal desires for white women and men (respectively), whites were ultimately responsible for miscegenation. Shyfeld's "careful, extensive and direct personal examinations"—his books were illustrated with photographs of naked black and mulatto men and women—led him to believe that there were many "degraded, sensuous white women" who chose "to copulate with black men, on account of the unusual length of time that the act commonly lasts with them and on account of the immensity of their parts."[16]

That Black Women Deliberately Set Out to Have
Sex with White Men

Edwin Brian Reuter's 1918 published doctoral dissertation, *The Mulatto in the United States*, was an important contribution to the hegemony of the University of Chicago's sociology department. Reuter had complicated speculations about the origin of the superiority of mulattoes among blacks that involved the "choicer" of black women deliberately seeking liaisons with low-class white men to further the life chances of their children among blacks.

These black mothers of mixed-race children, Reuter claimed, never objected to and generally sought out the interracial liaisons: "It was never at any time a matter of compulsion; on the contrary it was a matter of being honored by a man of a superior race. Speaking generally, the amount of inter-mixture is limited only by the self-respect of the white man and the compelling strength of the community sentiment."[17]

That Black Men Obsessively Lusted after White Women

This belief was the ultimate justification for the disenfranchisement of southern blacks, for segregation, and for the lynching of blacks, and at the turn of the century, it was a belief professed not merely by southern racist politicians but by educated southerners as well. Thus Ellen Barret Ligon, a physician in Mobile, Alabama, wrote in a 1903 *Good Housekeeping* article that black rapes of white women were a constant occurrence in the South: "The white woman is the coveted desire of the negro man. The despoiling of the white woman is his chosen vengeance. . . . The white woman must be saved."[18]

That It Was a Sin to Condone Miscegenation

In 1867, Buckner H. Payne, a Nashville publisher, referred to the Negro as a "pre-Adamite, created before Adam and Eve," and "a *separate* and *distinct* species of the *genus homo*." Payne believed that the biblical flood had been a punishment for the intermarriage between Adam's sons and the "inferior ape-like species."[19] This belief in divine retribution for miscegenation was a theme that ran through the racial paranoia of the post-Reconstruction South— some southerners believed that their defeat in the Civil War and subsequent hard times were a divine punishment for the racial mixing that had taken place during slavery.[20] Payne believed that equality between the races would lead to miscegenation (another racist theme of the times), which would bring down cataclysmic divine wrath: "The states and people that favor this equality and amalgamation of the white and black races, *God will exterminate.* A man cannot commit so great an offense against his race, against his country, against his God, . . . as to give his daughter in marriage to a negro-a-*beast*.[21]

That Miscegenation Was Unpatriotic because It Was a Danger to All That Was Fine in American Culture

Edward Drinker Cope, a zoologist and paleontologist at the University of Pennsylvania, was a strong proponent of the hierarchy of the races, and he held that at the bottom of this hierarchy the Negro "approximated to the ape." In 1870 he wrote that miscegenation was a "shameful sacrifice" for whites:

> We cannot cloud or extinguish the fine nervous susceptibility, and the mental force, which cultivation develops in the constitution of the Indo-European, by the fleshy instincts, and the dark mind of the African. Not only is the mind stagnated, and the life of mere living introduced in its stead, but the possibility of resurrection is rendered doubtful or impossible. The greatest danger which flows from the presence of the negro in this country, is the certainty of the contamination of the race.[22]

In *1956*, Herbert Ravenal Sass, writing for the *Atlantic Monthly*, equated mixed schools with "mixed blood":

> Many well-meaning persons have suddenly discovered that tenets of the Christian religion and the professions of our democratic faith compel us to accept the risks of hybridization. No one who will face up to the biological facts and really think the problem through can believe any such thing or see the partial suicide of the white race in America (and of the Negro race also) as anything other than a crime against both religion and civilization.[23]

In 1960 a federal judge inveighed against miscegenation in an *obiter dictum* that associated the political instability of Cuba and Haiti, as well as an assassination attempt by a Puerto Rican, with miscegenation. And in 1965 a congressman from Alabama read it into the *Congressional Record* that the miscegenistic aims of civil rights marchers in Montgomery were "communist-instigated."[24]

In a way, the vituperation against interracial sex fizzled out when it came to overt attacks against the "issue" of these tabooed acts. For a time at the turn of the century, there was a popular belief that most crimes committed by Negroes were committed by individuals of mixed race. But there is no documentation of direct persecution of individuals of black and white mixed race in the United States—perhaps because they were categorized as Negro or black. Rather, it was the images of mixed-race individuals in the American mind between the Civil War and World War I that were genocidal. The genocidal aspect of these images crystallized around what Williamson refers to as the "muleology" of the New South, the belief that people of mixed race were biologically incapable of perpetuating themselves. This muleology was crudely expressed in jokes that a mulatto had no ancestors and no descendants.[25] But the jokes were merely the vernacular form of scientific dogma.

The images of mixed race were in part derived from the prevailing assumptions about the "inferior" black race compared to the "superior" white race. The prevailing scientific theories of mixed-race individuals that were developed and refined after the Civil War had virtually no empirical base beyond anthropometric data concerning the brain weight and lung capacity of Civil War soldiers of mixed race, which had been collected by the Provost Marshal-General's Bureau and the U.S. Sanitary Commission.[26] And the development of scientific theory was accompanied by the political disenfranchisement and ostracization from white society of the emancipated black slaves and their descendants. But few writers blame the scientific literature for the oppression in the culture at large, for the simple reason that politicians and lynch mobs do not form their ideologies on the basis of what pass for learned treatises. Some writers attempt to excuse the scientists on the grounds that no intellectuals function outside of cultural contexts.[27] But whatever one's position on these contextual fine points, it seems judicious to view the entire late nineteenth- and early twentieth-century American social, political, and scientific historical context as virulently racist against blacks by the standards of contemporary emancipatory discussion.

The paradigm of American race theory was that humanity was divided into three or five major races, each of which had originated in a different geographical area on the planet. Each race was believed to have its own essence, or "genius," which was physically inherited by individuals of that race and carried in their blood. This racial essence was the bearer of cultural traits as well as physical characteristics. There had been a Darwinian struggle among all races and the most fit race had risen to dominance. The most fit race was the white race. The non-white races were inherently inferior to the white race.[28] That was the paradigm.

Within the paradigm of American race theory, there was a minor dispute among the monogeneticists and the polygeneticists about whether all of mankind had originated from one original race or whether there had always been separate and distinct races. But this dispute turned more on the question of whether Lamarkian-type adjustments to different geographical environments or inherent racial differences had caused the physical and cultural differences among the modern races. The monogenetic–polygenetic dispute did not turn on whether changes in environment could correct the presumed inferiority of the black race. Thus the Reverend A. W. Pitzer said, at an 1890 conference on "The Negro Problem," "The wild, naked, man-eating savages of equatorial Africa are of the same blood as the Negro of this Republic."[29] And Paul B. Barringer, chairman of the faculty at the University of Virginia, wrote in 1900, "If you scratch a Negro you will find a savage . . . the life history is the repetition of the race history . . . the life history of any individual, of any type, unless modified by forces of an exceptional character, will tend to conform to the lines of ancestral traits.[30]

The American social sciences began their academic life on the assumption that the accepted racial paradigm was true. Thus, in 1910, George Oscar Ferguson, a psychologist at the University of Virginia, began to publish data from intelligence testing that supported the theory of black inferiority.[31] It wasn't until the 1920s that Franz Boas's efforts to distinguish between biological heredity and acquired culture began to break down the old theory that blood was the carrier of cultural characteristics. Of course, some biologists had known since the turn of the century that blood types varied independently of racial characteristics.[32] But it took many years for this information to circulate through the social sciences, much less through ordinary language, if it has even to this day. Nonetheless, with the 1911 publication of *The Mind of Primitive Man*, Boas laid the foundation for the view that accident and environment were as important in shaping culture as was race. His insistence that the differences in mental ability and vitality within each race were as great as the differences between the "average types" of each race was a crucial attack on the old blood theory of culture.[33]

But the blood theory was remarkably persistent. In 1943, Ashly Montagu still found it necessary to inform readers that maternal and fetal blood circulate separately and that blood transfusions do not transmit racial characteristics.[34] In 1944 a public opinion poll found Americans equally divided among those who thought Negro and white blood were the same, those who thought that Negro blood was different from white blood, and those who did not know.[35] At present, many educated and progressive-thinking writers still use the term 'blood' in studying race, especially the term 'mixed blood.'

Indeed, it was the idea that mulattoes had mixed blood that stigmatized them in American history. This mixed blood was associated with physical debility, mental inferiority, and moral degeneracy. The association between mixed race and these negative characteristics not only incorporated the presumed-inferior racial characteristics of blacks, on account of the one-drop rule, but went several steps beyond racist beliefs about blacks. In an age that adored biological classification and seemed to derive human ontology from theories of "types" and "kinds," people of mixed race were denied this biological foundationism. Mulattoes were not accorded a solid existence physically, culturally, or morally; they were despised and dismissed, forms of devaluation that were more destructive in principle than direct hatred and denigration. It is difficult to imagine how any American of mixed race could feel assured of an ordinary existence as a person of mixed race after having been exposed to the prevailing scientific and popular images of mulattoness in the late nineteenth century.

What did it mean physically to be a mulatto according to nineteenth-century scientific speculation? First of all, one would have come into the world in violation of laws of nature that kept all species of animals within their own kinds for breeding purposes.[36] Physically, one would be something of a freak of nature. If one were a woman, one would be more prone to illness and more delicate than other women; if a man, more likely to contract tuberculosis and scrofulous diseases than other men.[37] In either case, one would be unlikely to live to old age. If one did live to old age and one had married another mulatto and one's children also married mulattoes, one's grandchildren would almost certainly be unable to reproduce.[38] One would not have the vitality of either one's black or one's white forebears. This would be partly due to a hypothetical neurological defect shared by all mulattoes. Neurologists claimed there were electrical currents in the human body that flowed in one direction in black people and in the opposite direction in white people. In people of mixed race, these currents were jumbled and confused, leading to all manner of physical ailments, not to mention mental confusion and overall flightiness.[39]

These physical defects were not postulated as the result of speculation but were offered as conclusions based on data observed by medical practitioners with long years of experience. In 1883, W. A. Dixon reported decades of such observations in an Ohio border community, and his prognoses about mixed race were uniformly negative:

> Those of the first cross were robust; those of the second were paler, more ashlike in complexion, of slender form, plainly bearing many of the characteristics of predisposition or inevitable tendencies to special diseases, of the strumous type. The third union resulted in less fertility and greater predisposition to disease. Now the children present the scrofulous physiognomy. The fourth union, still less fertile than the others, brings forth a progeny largely suffering from cutaneous affections, ophthalmia, rickets, dropsy of the head, white swelling of the knee joints, morbus coxrius, diseased glands, [and] suppurating sores until the whole generation is quite extinct.[40]

If one were a mulatto, one might be judged to be attractive in appearance on account of one's white physical characteristics, but people would call one "ring-tailed," "striped," "yellow," and perhaps a "yellow nigger." One would be considered unfit for manual labor, and one would be expected to have a strong aversion to the direct midday sun or perhaps to any bright sunlight.[41]

How would a person of mixed race be characterized mentally in the late nineteenth century? One would be expected to be more intelligent than a black person with no white ancestors. But one would not, no matter one's education or cultural attainments, be considered as intelligent as a white person.[42] And, of course, one's mind would be flighty!

What about the mulatto's cultural location in nineteenth-century America? According to the prevailing racial theory, as "neither fish nor fowl" mulattoes were bereft of culture in the sense in which culture was (assumed to be) based on a race and on the traditions of that race.[43] Therefore, it was held that mulattoes had no culture to speak of, because black culture was inferior to white culture and they had inherited that culture according to the one-drop rule. Mulattoes often showed the benefits of white culture, but this was thought to be merely a skill of mimicry expressing their deep desire to be white. The only cultural attainment that mulattoes were allowed was to be agitators on behalf of racial equality. This would come to them in their positions of leadership among blacks, but it would be no more than another expression of the deep confusion in the mulatto soul.

What was the nineteenth-century moral appraisal of mulattoes? Many white racists believed that mulattoes were morally degenerate on account of their degenerate origins, and this in spite of—or as a diabolical twist to—the fact that so many people of mixed race were teachers and ministers.[44] Blacks were always suspicious of mulattoes, especially mulattoes who came from old exclusive families that had been free before the Civil War. According to the black stereotype, these mulattoes kept themselves aloof from other blacks and thought they were superior to them.[45] In the twentieth century, after the old mulatto elite had disintegrated and miscegenation was on the decline among the more respectable classes in society, E. Franklin Frazier presented this description of mixed-race morality in one of his "zones" of the black community in Chicago in the 1930s (where one out of three men and two out of five women showed mixed ancestry):

Through the heart of this zone ran Thirty-fifth Street, the bright-light area of the Negro community. Here we found the "black and tan" cabarets, pleasure gardens, gambling places, night clubs, hotels, and houses of prostitution. It was the headquarters of the famous "policy king"; the rendezvous of the "pretty" brown-skinned boys, many of whom were former bell-hops, who "worked" white and colored girls in hotels and on the streets; here the mulatto queen of the underworld ran the biggest poker game on the South Side; here the "gambler de luxe" ruled until he was killed by a brow-beaten waiter. In this world the mulatto girl from the South, who ever since she heard that she was "pretty enough to be an actress," had visions of the stage, realized her dream in one of the cheap theaters. To this same congenial environment the mulatto boy from Oklahoma, who danced in the role of the son of an Indian woman, had found his way. To this area were attracted the Bohemian, the disorganized, and the vicious elements in the Negro world.[46]

The final genocidal cast to images of mixed race in both nineteenth- and twentieth-century America involves neither condemnation of miscegenation nor fear of it but a tone of reassurance. Since the Civil War there have been repeated assurances that miscegenation is on the wane. Sometimes the assurance comes from whites and sometimes from blacks. In the context of discussions about the dangers of miscegenation or concern for the plight of mixed-race individuals—a concern that is seldom expressed—the repeated prediction that there will be less miscegenation in the future always implies that this will be a welcomed solution to an onerous problem created in the past. And this is a "final solution" if ever there was one: "Don't worry, the day is coming when there will be no more of *them*." The prediction that miscegenation will decrease in the future may be welcomed by blacks and whites in a biracial society. But such a prediction never addresses those of mixed race who already exist or those of mixed race who will be born after the prediction has been made.

After the Civil War the Knights of the White Camellia, the Ku Klux Klan, and proud black patriarchs were effective in curtailing the minor increase in interracial marriages that had begun during

Reconstruction.[47] When southerners spoke of the abhorrence of miscegenation in the 1890s, they were confident that most whites understood they were degrading themselves if they bred with blacks. Atticus G. Haywood, a Methodist bishop, thought that blacks as well as whites were entitled to some of the credit for the decline of miscegenation in the postbellum South: "It is absolutely settled that the tendencies against miscegenation increase in both races. Fewer mulattoes are born each year. The moral tone of the Negroes does improve. The white man recoils from amalgamation more than in former days; and law teaches all."[48]

Recent writers, discussing mixed race within the context of the one-drop rule, have spread the same reassurance. Thus Joel Williamson, writing in the late 1970s, alluded to an increase in interracial marriages after the 1960s civil rights movement but cited sources to the effect that interracial marriages were less than 1 percent of all marriages, a rate that he thought not likely to increase.[49] Beth Day, writing in the early 1970s, anticipated Williamson. Day's book *Sexual Life between Blacks and Whites* was supportive of interracial marriage as a solution to American racism. (Her introduction was written by Margaret Mead, who was a student of Franz Boas.) But Day, like Williamson, accepted the one-drop rule.[50] It is therefore difficult to see how her solution amounts to anything beyond the solution of the Harlem Renaissance, even though her solution is statistically insignificant by her own reckoning.

In fact, both Day and Williamson were mistaken in their predictions. The U.S. census data for 1991 would seem to place interracial marriages in the United States at close to 2 percent of all marriages. And since 1968, interracial births have risen twenty-six times faster than the overall birth rate.[51] But can it be only numbers that give a minority the right to a separate racial identity in a society that attaches great importance to racial identity? Granted, if there were no people of mixed race in the United States, the problem of their identity would not arise. But as long as there are any, have they not the same right, if it is a question of rights, to a racial identity as do blacks and whites?

$$\boxed{12}$$

Mulattoes
in Fiction

When all else fails in what must be accepted as the real world, it is sometimes possible to look to art for redemption. Thus far no historical basis for an American identity of mixed race has emerged: There is no legal tradition that supports the existence of mixed racial categories; there have been no enduring communities of mixed-race individuals; there is no value-positive tradition of mixed-race descriptions in science or folklore; and the black emancipatory tradition rejects the possibility of a mixed-race people or segment of society, as finally as does the white tradition of racial purity. But people of mixed race have always existed in the United States. Therefore the next step is to turn to literature, in case American writers, especially those who have been otherwise acclaimed, have had anything positive to say about Americans of mixed race. The search here is not for literary values but for images in texts with which it would be liberating or in any way constructive for a person of mixed race to identify. Perhaps there is an optimism in artistic traditions that has eluded science and politics. Or, it might be that Friedrich Nietzsche's warning against artists will be relevant:

> They do not stand nearly independently enough in the world and *against* the world for their changing valuations to deserve attention *in themselves*! They have at all times been valets of some morality, philosophy or religion; quite apart from the fact that they have unfortunately been all-too-pliable courtiers of their own followers and patrons, and cunning flatterers of ancient or newly arrived powers. They always need at the very least protec-

tion, a prop, an established authority: artists never stand apart; standing alone is contrary to their deepest instincts.[1]

American fiction with mixed-race protagonists can be divided into conventionally plotted Victorian stories written before the twentieth century and a smaller number of less didactic modern works. This discussion begins with a summary of the major themes and motifs of the early writings; special note is then taken of the special case of Mark Twain; and the concluding focus is on details of the valuation of mixed race in works by James Weldon Johnson, Jean Toomer, William Faulkner, and Toni Morrison.

As a source of historical information, the subject of mixed race in American literature can be approached from several frameworks. For example, Gary Wintz divides the material into fiction by black writers and fiction by white writers.[2] According to James Kinney, miscegenation, or amalgamation—"the process of combining mercury with another metal to form an alloy"—can be viewed as a recurrent trope in popular fiction, a sort of metaphor for the unblended part of the melting pot of American society as a whole; the problems of all black Americans in white American culture; or the alienation of the modern human in general.[3] Characters of mixed race have also been interpreted as universal cultural archetypes, such as the scapegoat or Christ figure (in Faulkner's work, for example).[4] But the concern here is the more narrow question of whether mixed-race fictional characters have a (positive) racial identity distinct from black or white.

In the nineteenth century, most novelists accepted the scientific and popular dogma that racial essences inhered in individuals and made them black or white. It was not merely a culturally debased heritage of slavery that blacks were presumed to carry but "six thousand years of savagery and mental dimness." Not only could his racial "genius" of blackness dominate an individual through one drop of black blood, but the blackness of someone who appeared white but who had the one drop was infinitely transitive. The white one-dropper in a marriage with a purely white no-dropper could be responsible for the creation of a racially "atavistic" child, as in this fear depicted by a black writer: "They say,

THE HISTORY OF MIXED RACE

Wanda, that the offspring of a quagga and a mare will have its mark,—will be striped. . . . Some people call me a quagga. . . . We must live apart, dearest; I cannot ruin your life because mine is ruined."[5] There was also the purely fictional fantasy of a visibly black child born to a one-dropper and a no-dropper, as expressed in white racist literature:

> It was a negro baby: the colour that was of Ethiopia, the unmistakeable nose, the hair that curled so tightly, the lips that were African, the large whites of the eyes. Verily a negro baby: and yet in an indefinable way a likeness of Helen, a caricature of Helen, a horrible travesty of Helen's features in combination with whose? Not Hayward Graham's. But whose, then? Helen's and whose? . . . Mr. Phillips could not answer his own question—he had never seen Guinea Gumbo [Guinea Gumbo being a depraved black ancestor of the baby's light mulatto father].[6]

Both black and white nineteenth-century literature employed the tragedy of the mulatto, a stereotype of situations as well as individuals. In abolitionist fiction, white-appearing slaves were sometimes sold into slavery by relatives after the death of white fathers who had freed them. Sometimes it was the white fathers who sold their own mixed-race children into slavery.[7] After the Civil War, the tragic mulatto became the noble mulatto who gave up the opportunity to pass for white in order to benefit less culturally privileged, darker-skinned, designated black people. In fiction written by blacks, duty and decency required that the person of mixed race identify with blacks.[8] In fiction written by whites, it always ruined the life of a person of mixed race, who believed in a purely white ancestry, to discover the existence of a black ancestor.[9]

The tragic or noble mulatto was often graced with unusual physical attractiveness. In black literature the attractiveness of women of mixed race could be presented as an ethereal bodily expression of their noble characters.[10] In white liberal literature the beauty of such women was part of the tragic contradiction of their situation—they could not marry white men or be accepted in refined white society even though everything else about them suggested that they should.[11] In white racist novels the attractive quadroon or octoroon was an unscrupulous, animalistic temptress who used her primitive charms to corrupt and ruin otherwise innocent white men.[12] Mixed-race male heroes were also variously doomed, noble, and menacing, depending on the ideology of the writer. Like his female counterpart, when he was good the male mulatto embodied moral courage, altruism, moral purity, and the added masculine virtue of being a good provider.[13] When he was bad, the male mulatto was an African savage who was obsessed with the carnal possession of white women.[14]

After Reconstruction the subject of passing became an absorbing theme in popular fiction. Often, passing was treated more pragmatically by white writers than in black literature. Thus in *An Imperative Duty* by William Dean Howells, the white Dr. Olney tells his future wife that she might have a duty to identify with blacks if

> you had voluntarily chosen your part with them—if you had ever *consented* to be of their kind. Then it *would* be base and cowardly to desert them; it would be a treason of the vilest sort. But you never did that, or anything like it, and there is no more specific obligation upon you to give your life to their elevation than there is upon me. Besides, I doubt if that sort of specific devotion would do much good. The way to elevate them is to elevate *us*, to begin with. It will be an easier matter to deal with those simple-minded folks after we've got the right way ourselves.[15]

Those black writers who were tolerant toward passing, such as Charles Chesnutt, emphasized the social chasms between uneducated poor blacks and more privileged light-skinned blacks. Chesnutt was a strong spokesman for racial justice, but personally he found it distasteful to live among poor blacks in the South—he has been sharply criticized for snobbishness and a desire to substitute class distinctions for racial ones.[16]

The most critically detached stance toward the one-drop rule and mixed race in American fiction can be found in Mark Twain's *The Tragedy of Pudd'nhead Wilson*. Critics have debated Twain's underlying racial ideology in this dialectical treatment of biology and society, but the simple reading and the one most appropriate to Mark Twain is that he was patronizing the racism of his readers.[17]

The plot of *Pudd'nhead Wilson* is a masterwork of ironies: Roxy, a slave who is descended from aristocratic Virginians with one black great-great-grandparent—she is "one-sixteenth" black— gives birth to a son by her master on the same day that her master's wife also bears a son. The wife dies and Roxy switches the babies. Tom, who is "one-thirty-second" black, is raised by his cruel, vicious father as the white heir, and Chambers, the real heir, grows up as a slave. Tom grows up uncaring and arrogant, and Chambers develops into a servile slave. Roxy is a survivor, with no pride in her black ancestry. Tom mistreats both Roxy and Chambers. When Tom's father dies, Roxy is freed and goes away for eight years. Upon her return, she tells Tom that he is one- thirty-second black. After an initial shock, Tom decides that his racial ancestry does not matter as long as no one else knows about it. He sells Roxy down the river. She escapes and demands that he buy her freedom. Tom robs and kills his uncle for the money. Both his guilt in this crime and his black designation are discov- ered by the town crank, Pudd'nhead Wilson, who had finger- printed Tom and Chambers when they were infants. Chambers be- comes the heir, and Tom is sold down the river.

As James Kinney observes, while it is obvious that Mark Twain thought that environment was more important than racial essence in shaping character, it is discomforting that Roxy blames Tom's failures on his "drop" of "nigger blood." It is also discom- forting to a modern reader that Tom meets the fate dictated by the one-drop rule. However, Kinney also points out that Roxy's rac- ism is similar to Huckleberry Finn's when he helps his friend Jim escape—Roxy and Huck are "unreliable" narrators, intended to be read at a distance from the author himself.[18]

Indeed, Huck renounces the conventional morality of his day in order to rationalize his good deed—he is willing to give up all morality, if necessary. In an article about the conscience of Huck- leberry Finn that has received stellar attention in the literature of contemporary moral philosophy (although not specifically for its treatment of race), Jonathan Bennett insists that there are times when compassion ought to be more important than one's accepted moral code.[19] It is now difficult to view the property rights of slave owners as a consideration in a moral code, but Huckleberry Finn sincerely did. And Roxy just as sincerely believed that one drop of black blood was sufficient to cause essential moral inferiority, in this case, Tom's bad character. Unlike Huck, Roxy did not slough off her society's morality about race. But Tom did, and in this he arrived at an accurate assessment of race—that it is a social fiction. However, he came to this conclusion from motives of pure self-interest. Tom is a moral mirror image of Huck: Huck acted correctly but did not see things clearly; Tom saw things clearly but did not act correctly.

In theory, *Pudd'nhead Wilson* offers a rational solution to the American problem of one-drop mixed race. The solution is that the only empirical meaning a category such as race can have is as a reference to an individual's physical appearance: If a person with a black forebear looks white, then that person is white. This is Tom's solution to his problem of mixed race, that his black forebear is of no importance except in the minds of other people. But only people of mixed race who look completely white are addressed by this solution. Nothing is suggested about how the race of a person who looks as if he or she has both black and white forebears ought to be considered. We now know that a person who looks white and who has a black forebear may have no racial genes from that black forebear, that is, such a person might be purely white genetically. Mark Twain may or may not have realized this biological fact of heredity, but whether or not he did could not clarify how he might have extended his solution to individuals who *appeared* to be of mixed race.

After the turn of the century, novelists focused on the psychology of mixed-race characters, and mixed-race situations were depicted even more bleakly. James Weldon Johnson developed a complex point of view from the standpoint of a mixed-race protagonist, which was resolved into a longing for black identity that anticipated the Harlem Renaissance. Johnson's fictional narrator in *The Autobiography of an Ex-Colored Man* is brought up gently by his black mother, who loves his white southern father. When his mother dies, he is adrift in the world until a millionaire friend rescues him in Harlem and takes him on the Grand Tour of Europe. The protagonist's longing for black racial identity brings him back to the American South when he resolves to document black folk music. But he is so traumatized by witnessing a lynching that he decides to "raise a mustache" and allow people to take him for white. He gives up his art and marries a white woman who loves him. She dies and he devotes himself to making money and raising his children. At the end of the narrative, Johnson's protagonist picks up his black identity by explicitly regretting the loss of it. Like W.E.B. Du Bois, he seems to believe that there is a black racial essence that needs to be expressed in an important cultural destiny. The truth for him is that he feels he has sold his "birthright for a mess of pottage." He regrets not being part of

> that small but gallant band of coloured men who are publicly fighting the cause of their race. . . . Even those who oppose them know that these men have the eternal principles of right on their side, and they will be victors even though they should go down in defeat. Beside them I feel small and selfish. I am an ordinarily successful white man who has made a little money. They are men who are making history and a race. I, too, might have taken part in a work so glorious.[20]

It should be noted that Johnson seems to be saying here that black racial identity is something that must be created rather than discovered. Also, he refers to the black leaders he admires as "making . . . a race." If that phrase is taken literally, it has implications for breeding, i.e., choices in human reproduction as well as the non-eugenic products of culture. As to the question of mixed race, Johnson does not ever consider it. His protagonist has become white as an alternative to black. Period.

In one of Jean Toomer's vignettes in *Cane*, Paul, a mixed-race character, experiences white perceptions of his appearance. First, the stares of white patrons in a dinner club irritate Paul's white friend, Art:

> Crimson Gardens. Hurrah! So one feels.
> People . . . University of Chicago students, members of the stock exchange, a large Negro in crimson uniform who guards

the door . . . had watched them enter. Had leaned towards each
other over ash-smeared tablecloths and high-balls and whispered:
What is he, a Spaniard, an Indian, an Italian, a Mexican, Hindu,
or a Japanese? Art had at first fidgeted under their stares . . .
what are *you* looking at, you godam [*sic*] pack of owl-eyed hy-
enas? . . . but soon settled into his fuss with Helen, and forgot
them.

But after Art forgets about it, Paul, left on his own, becomes
aware of his difference from whites in a way that puts him at ease,
because earlier on he had been marveling at their difference from
him:

A strange thing happened to Paul. Suddenly he knew that he was
apart from the people around him. Apart from the pain which
they had unconsciously caused. Suddenly he knew that people
saw, not attractiveness in his dark skin, but difference. Their
stares giving him to himself, filled something long empty within
him and were like green blades sprouting in his consciousness.
There was fullness, and strength and peace about it all. He saw
himself, cloudy, but real. He saw the faces of the people at the
tables around him. White light, or as now, the pink lights of the
Crimson Gardens gave a glow and immediacy to white faces.
The pleasure of it, equal to that of love or dream, of seeing this.
Art and Bona and Helen? He'd look. They were wonderfully
flushed and beautiful. Not for himself; because they were. Dis-
tantly. Who were they, anyway? God, if he knew them. He'd
come in with them. Of that he was sure. Come where? Into life?
Yes. No. Into the Crimson Gardens. A part of life. A carbon
bubble. Would it look purple if he went out and into the night
and looked at it? His sudden starting to rise almost upset the
table.[21]

When Paul wonders if the Crimson Gardens will look purple if
he goes outside and looks at it as a whole, this is a reference to his
earlier perception of the difference of white people from him:

Paul, contrary to what he had thought he would be like, is cool
like the dusk, and like the dusk, detached. His dark face is a
floating shade in evening's shadow. He sees Art, curiously. Art
is a purple fluid, carbon-charged, that effervesces besides him.
He loves Art. But is it not queer, this pale purple facsimile of a

red-blooded Norwegian friend of his? Perhaps for some reason, white skins are not supposed to live at night. Surely, enough nights would transform them fantastically, or kill them. And their red passion? Night paled that too and made it moony.[22]

Toomer's emphasis on difference anticipates a modern line of thought that comes to full expression with Jacques Derrida and his commentators and critics.[23] If one does not interpret certain physical characteristics as racial characteristics but nonetheless notices how others interpret such characteristics as racial, a perception of *difference* (or *différance*), can result. Franz Fanon also captured this sense of *difference* when he wrote about a child expressing alarm at the sight of him: "Mama, see the Negro! I'm frightened."[24] Although the child was reacting with the prejudice which it had been taught, Fanon was experiencing himself as *different* because he knew that the child had to begin with a perception of his difference.

The *difference* of Paul (Toomer's character) is the same in principle as the *difference* noted by Fanon. Paul's *difference* is not apparent to the white (or purple) onlookers who interpret certain of his physical characteristics which differ from theirs as racial characteristics.[25] Thus, the starers speculate that Paul is an exotic foreigner of some "kind," and their need to categorize him makes him aware of his *difference*, because he knows that if they categorize him "correctly" they would vilify him as his friend Art's girlfriend, Eliza, has done:

> O Eliza . . . rabbit-eyes sparkling, plays up to, and tries to placate what she considers to be Paul's contempt. She always does that . . . Little Liza Jane . . . Once home she burns with the thought of what she's done. She says all manner of snidy things about him, and swears that she'll never go out again when he is along. She tries to get Art to break with him, saying, that if Paul, whom the whole dormitory call a nigger, is more to him than she is, well she's through.[26]

Only a person of a race other than the race of his observers could experience other people's perceptions of his difference from them as Fanon and Paul do. That Paul is of mixed race in prejudiced but not murderously racist white society allows him the peace to relax into his own identity as he does in the Crimson Gardens. Paul is then relieved to accept his *difference* even though it is not clear to him what this *difference* should mean racially: "He saw himself cloudy but real."

Toomer has here sketched a phenomenology of physical racial perception, from the viewpoint of a person of mixed black and white race who is passing with tolerable but not complete success in American society. Toomer's self-description—"cloudy but real"—is the beginning of an identity of mixed race, from the standpoint of mixed race, in literature. It takes up exactly where Mark Twain left off in addressing the position of the person of mixed race who does not look completely white. But his beginning is fragmented, and Toomer himself did not leave us anything more.

Mixed race was a persistent theme for William Faulkner. However, Faulkner's writings are inconclusive about any coherent solution to the problem, and there is also doubt about the extent to which Faulkner himself believed some of the racist racial myths of the South.[27] Faulkner dealt obsessively and at times complicitously with failed close relationships, through themes of incest, illegitimacy, and violence—all mixed up with miscegenation. But when events got larger than ordinary life in his fiction, he had a tendency to mythologize. The following description of Joe Christmas's death is unfortunate, because the blood that flows from his castrated groin is called "black" by Faulkner, and no one knows exactly what Joe's race is all through *Light in August*:

> "Now you'll let white women alone, even in hell," he said. But the man on the floor had not moved. He just lay there, with his eyes open and empty of everything save consciousness, and with something, a shadow, about his mouth. For a long moment he looked up at them with peaceful and unfathomable and unbearable eyes. Then his face, body, all, seemed to collapse, to fall in upon itself, and from out the slashed garments about his hips and loins the pent up black blood seemed to rush like a released breath. It seemed to rush out of his pale body like the rush of sparks from a rising rocket; upon that black blast the man seemed to rise soaring into their memories forever and ever.[28]

There is mythology in the term 'black blood' and mythology in the suggestion that Joe Christmas will loom over his murderers long after he is dead. These conceptually extravagant mythologies of blood and memory frustrate all attempts to consider or understand mixed race in particular individual lives—the blood of victims, no matter what "color," does not have the "power" to immortalize them in the minds of their murderers; and even if it did, the world would not necessarily be a gentler place.

In *Absalom, Absalom!*, Charles Etienne De Saint Velery Bon, who is "one-sixteenth" black, goes to live with a white and a mulatto step-aunt in Mississippi after the death of his New Orleans Quadroon mother, who had raised him in coddled luxury. The aunts try to protect Charles, but the outside world continually threatens him with violence until he marries a very dark-skinned woman and turns his back on any claims to whiteness, becoming a tenant farmer. He dies of illness at a young age, leaving a son who is undeniably black and content to farm.

Faulkner's depictions of southern mulattoes are tragic to the point of horror, but the tragedy always moves away from the individual in question to become a mythopoeic aspect of southern society. In that sense, Faulkner contributes little to a mixed-race point of view. Rather, the topic is of interest within his fiction because of what he, as the powerful artist he was, did with it—the topic of mixed race is of interest within Faulkner's writing because of what it did for him as an artist. There is another caveat about artists from Friedrich Nietzsche that is relevant here: "Whoever is completely and wholly an artist is to all eternity separated from the 'real,' the actual."[29]

With the exception of Mark Twain and perhaps Charles Chesnutt, the nineteenth-century writers who addressed the issue of mixed race did so conventionally, in accordance with the one-drop rule, regardless of whether they were black or white. In the twentieth century, with the exception of Toomer's fragments, the refusal to recognize what can only be called the right to exist of individuals of mixed race has been even more absolute than it was in nineteenth-century novels. This refusal is especially ironic when it is expressed by a black writer. For example, in *The Bluest Eye*, written in 1970, Toni Morrison depicts mulattoes as malevolently destructive to the well-being of black people. This depiction reflects some of the worst racist fears of miscegenation from a black point of view.

Morrison's heroine, Pecola Breedlove, is an eleven-year-old, poor black girl. Pecola is ugly by conventional standards of white, "brown," and perhaps even black beauty. Pecola's father rapes and impregnates her. Pecola finally takes refuge in insanity, but not before the reader has had every opportunity to empathize with her position on the bottom of the racist society that has made even blacks racist against blackness. Somehow Pecola's father is presumed not to be entirely at fault for raping her, on account of what he has himself endured.[30] Pecola's mother, whom her own children call "Mrs. Breedlove," clearly treats the white little girl in whose house she works as a maid with more tenderness than she does her own daughter.[31] Maureen Peal, "a high yellow dream child with long brown hair braided into two lynch ropes," torments Pecola because she is black and has seen her father naked.[32] Geraldine, a "brown" middle-class housewife with bourgeois white values, throws Pecola out of her house when her own spoiled son has unjustly blamed her for the death of a pet cat, which he tortured after luring Pecola into the house in the first place: "'Get out,' she said, her voice quiet. 'You nasty little black bitch. Get out of my house.'"[33]

But the person who finally pushes Pecola over the brink is a stereotyped, decadent scion of a mulatto elite family in the West Indies. This is Elihue Whitcomb, known in Pecola's neighborhood as "Soaphead Church." Whitcomb is something of a spiritual advisor to depressed people, a religious charlatan who loves old, worn things and molests little girls. Pecola goes to him in the depth of her despair to ask him to turn her brown eyes blue. He gives her a piece of meat laced with poison to feed to his landlady's diseased old dog, Bob. He loathes Bob but is too disgusted by him to get close enough to him to kill him himself. Whitcomb tells Pecola that if Bob does anything unusual after eating the meat, it will be a sign from God that her eyes have turned blue. The dog goes into death throes, Pecola enters irreversible insanity, and Soaphead

Church writes a long letter to God, which may be a suicide note. Morrison tells the reader throughout this episode that Whitcomb's problems are a result of his breeding:

> He had been reared in a family proud of its academic accomplishments and its mixed blood—in fact, they believed the former was based on the latter. . . .
>
> With the confidence born of a conviction of superiority, they performed well at schools. They were industrious, orderly, and energetic, hoping to prove beyond a doubt De Gobineau's hypothesis that "all civilizations derive from the white race, that none can exist without its help, and that a society is great and brilliant only so far as it preserves the blood of the noble group that created it." Thus, they were seldom overlooked by schoolmasters who recommended promising students for study abroad. The men studied medicine, law, theology, and emerged repeatedly in the powerless government offices available to the native population. That they were corrupt in public and private practice, both lecherous and lascivious, was considered their noble right, and thoroughly enjoyed by most of the less gifted population.
>
> Little Elihue learned everything he needed to know well, particularly the fine art of self-deception.[34]

It is not clear in what Morrison locates Whitcomb's self-deception. The suggestion is strong that this is neither an ordinary psychological inability to deal with reality nor a racially neutral character defect. Rather, the reader is urged to conclude that the root of Whitcomb's self-deception, as well as the basis of the evil he wreaks, is his denial that he is black. Somehow his denial of his blackness is more blameworthy than Mrs. Breedlove's denial of her blackness—she favors her white employer's child over her own and psychically inhabits a world of stereotyped white ideals. Why is a person of mixed black and white race more to blame for self-denial of blackness than a person of "pure" black race? Morrison's condemnation of individuals of mixed race in this regard can be read only as a racial bias against such individuals. Morrison's bias makes sense only if she believes that there are no individuals of mixed black and white race and that all individuals who think they are so mixed are, in fact, light-skinned black people who have learned "the fine art of self-deception." Morrison has without question learned the fine art of writing tragedy, perhaps too well; for the *The Bluest Eye* perpetuates the tragedy of genocidal images of mixed race.

13

Alienation

There should be a clear answer to the question of how many Americans of mixed black and white race there are. It may seem that this question could be answered separately from the legal, scientific, cultural, and literary aspects of the matter of mixed race. However, the issue of numbers is logically intertwined with all of the other aspects of mixed race in American history: According to the one-drop rule for designated blackness, which was presented theoretically in Part I as the asymmetrical kinship schema of racial inheritance, there are no people of mixed race in the United States and there never have been. But if black and white races are posited as neutral biological categories, then those people who have both black and white forebears would all be of mixed black and white race. From this perspective, numbers can be calculated easily: Out of an estimated two hundred and fifty million Americans, 12 percent are designated black and something over 50 percent are designated white; some small percentage of those designated white have black ancestors; approximately 75 percent of those designated black have white ancestors. Therefore there are at least twenty million Americans of mixed black and white race.

However, any figure of mixed-race Americans is going to be out of phase with American cultural history. To belong to a race in the United States involves a shared past, recognition by other large groups of racially designated people, and some kind of community or ideal of solidarity—none of which exists or ever has existed for individuals who could be designated mixed black and white race.

Furthermore, ordinary language betrays the physical concept of race at the same time that it purports to intend it; for when Americans designate people racially, they include a reference to their culture, whether they believe that cultural traits are inherited or that they are learned after birth. And it is no less of a cultural reference when Americans insist that people of mixed race are black than when they refer to presumably pure-race people as black. The slight of reason in both cases is that race is acquired from the race of one's kin and that one's (cultural) heritage or inheritance from kin constitutes a genetic endowment.

The contemporary requirement that all speakers in emancipatory discourse identify themselves racially or ethnically remains as impossible for an American of mixed race to fulfill on the basis of the history of mixed race as it may be for many individuals to fulfill on the basis of their family histories. The conclusion to all of the foregoing inquiries into the history of mixed race in the United States can be summed up in one word: *alienation*.

The alienation of an American of mixed race is even itself alien. Normally, one is alienated if one is different from one's present surroundings because one has been separated from another place and culture in which one had been not-alienated or "natural." Thus the Jewish immigrant from Lithuania is an alien in Manhattan, alienated from her village outside Vilna; and the African slave brought to a Virginia plantation is alienated from his African community. But the American of mixed black and white race has no previous context from which he can be said to have been separated, so he is even alienated from normal forms of alienation.

One would think that, as a consolation for this alien alienation, it would be easier for an American of mixed race to forget about racial categories altogether. But though the psychological motives for such willed amnesia may be strong, social situations make it difficult to achieve. Most minorities, no matter how badly they are oppressed by the dominant society, have the option of forgetting about what it is that designates them as different while they are among other members of the same group. But an American of mixed black and white race is as strange to blacks as she is to whites, as soon as she insists on an identity of mixed race. Presumably, her racial condition is shared by those 19,999,999 other individuals of mixed race. But the awareness of the possibility of a mixed-race identity does not even exist as something that is commonly understood among those 19,999,999 people, because they have not yet been identified as mixed race in any way beyond genetic statistics. All racial identities that are constructed in the first person presuppose racial identifications that are made in the second or third person: To be able to experience myself as mixed race, someone has to tell me that I am mixed race or I need to identify with someone else who has been identified as mixed race. This is another way of saying that racial identities are subjective whereas racial identifications are objective.

Racial identities must be based on racial identifications because the ordinary concept of race is a cultural artifact that varies from place to place and time to time. There is nothing in the nature of consciousness or the phenomenology of human bodily experience which, in the absence of external identification, can constitute a racial identity. Racial identities therefore come after racial identifications. If black and white racial identifications are fundamentally unsound and unjust, as I have argued, then black and white racial identities which are based on those identifications are inherently unsound, unjust, false, or otherwise mistaken.

If an identity of mixed race could be put together out of black and white identities or, more directly, out of black and white identifications, something would be wrong with that as well. But the situation for people of mixed race is even more difficult. Their existence as mixed-race individuals is not recognized in the American biracial system. They are not identified as mixed race, they have no past family members who have been so identified and with whom they can identify, and there is no impersonal history of individuals of mixed race—all of the mixed-race people are black in the United States. It is therefore virtually impossible for individuals of mixed race, who should be acknowledged to exist, if races exist, but who are not so acknowledged, to have mixed-race identities. Why should an individual insist on such an identity?

One good reason for insisting on an identity of mixed race is that it is a way of resisting the racism inherent in American racial designations. Also, such an insistence makes sense within any logic of biological racial categories. But the obstacles to American mixed-race identity are formidable. James Weldon Johnson, at the close of *Autobiography of an Ex-Colored Man*, in 1912 visualized the black race as emergent, yet-to-be-made. If one wanted to create an identity of mixed race at this time in the United States, one would not even be at the point where Johnson thought the black race was in 1912! Most Americans of mixed black and white race do not even have an inkling that such a racial category could be thought.

To attempt to create a racial identity of mixed race, based on the history of mixed race in the United States, would involve not only many intensely deconstructive dialogues with past texts but positive reconstructions and constructions in racial theory and practice. It would take a long time and would require the consensus of large numbers of both black and white Americans. At this point, it is difficult to see how a commitment to such a project could provide the benefits that are normally associated with belonging to an ethnic group or a tradition.

When every solution to a problem fails, sometimes the problem itself must be questioned. Perhaps the fragmented, suppressed, denied, and alienated history of mixed race in the United States should raise questions about the value of any racial identity. What in theory is involved in racial and ethnic identities from the standpoint of one who *identifies*? Can it really be so much more difficult to identify oneself as *on* the line of black and white—Du Bois's famous "color line"—than it is to identify oneself with either side of it? Or are there problems in principle with any affirmation of personal identity as an identification with the "blood" of one's ancestors? American history has no answers to these questions. The questions themselves need to be clarified in philosophical frameworks, although to date no American philosopher has been concerned with such questions. Indeed, racial and ethnic theory has not been addressed as a topic within the broad Enlightenment traditions of the History of Philosophy, although, to be sure, many traditional philosophers have made racist remarks and argued on racist assumptions.[1] There is one striking exception to the conservative white European ethnocentric bias in Philosophy, and that is Jean-Paul Sartre. In Part III, therefore, the tentative and somewhat ambivalent conclusions to this work will begin with Sartre's critique of a uniquely French ethnocentricity: French anti-Semitism. It will be seen that Sartre's negative standard reveals a basic tension between human freedom and any racial identity.

But before turning to Sartre, something should be said about folk notions of racial identity, because they have been almost completely neglected in previous chapters and where they have been noted, the attention has been critical. This has been necessary in order to reconstruct American racial concepts into logical forms that could then be philosophically analyzed. The logical forms of racial identifications and identities have been criticized so that black and white racial identifications have been shown not to make sense in important ways and mixed-race identifications not to exist. However, this should not be read as a lack of respect for those folk racial identities, especially black ones, that people find meaningful and that are socially cohesive and consoling.

Folk racial identities are the *practice* of everyday life, and the analysis here is *theory*. Neither practice nor theory is sacrosanct or "written in stone," and no one can say which is more important or more "true." From the standpoint of theory, practice may look misguided, whereas from the standpoint of practice, theory may look superfluous. Practice and theory change each other on the ground of *ideology*. And practice and theory merge to become each other in those experiments of existence that could be called *praxis*. The emancipatory tradition that began with abolitionism in the United States is an example of ideology. Emancipation itself, desegregation, and contemporary affirmative action programs are all examples of praxis.

The folk identities of mixed-race Americans are complex, ambiguous, and ambivalent. They range from the dysfunctional and unentitled to the exotic and transcendent. On the face of it, whether they are identified by others as being of mixed race or not, Americans of mixed race have more racial freedom than either blacks or whites. They can construct and present themselves as black or white in the society of blacks or as black or white in the society of whites. They can conceal or reveal the race of their forebears, create racial mysteries around themselves, or refuse to see themselves in racial terms at all. Americans of mixed race can "pass" for either black or white, although everyone expects them to try to "be" black and many profess outrage if they present themselves as white (regardless of how many white kin they have).

The logic of successful passing for white by mixed-race individuals—and no one else can do it—precludes accurate documentation, just as does the logic of successful espionage. But degrees of passing can easily be imagined, from concealing black ancestry from casual acquaintances to lying to people who would be expected to know the race of one's forebears to self-deception—or any combination thereof, over a lifetime. The identification of someone of mixed race as someone who is able to pass for white, along with the presumption that it is morally wrong to do so, is a folk identification of mixed-race individuals as potentially phoney white. Third-person folk identification of mixed race sets up a folk moral identity that is at odds with conventional notions of respectability among whites and honor among blacks. It has the potential to be an identity of shame, guilt, and defiance, which most people would consider to be psychologically unhealthy.

Philosophically, a "passing" folk identity of mixed race registers as an instance of alienation. It is not the only instance of alienation that is experienced by Americans of mixed race, and it is not the only folk identity that they have. Zora Neale Hurston, for example, when she presents the facts about herself as a mixed-race individual, identifies herself without moral qualifications and encourages others to do the same: "I see no need to manufacture me a legend to beat the facts. I do not coyly admit to a touch of the tarbrush to my Indian and white ancestry. . . . I am a mixed blood, it is true . . . I maintain that I have been a Negro three times—a Negro baby, a Negro girl, and a Negro woman."[2]

But Hurston does not explain how, if she sees herself as mixed race, she can *logically* identify herself as a Negro/ To be sure, Hurston describes herself with charm; she not only has a folk identity but is a folk heroine. No philosophical analysis or excursion into racial theory can belittle her identity as a designated black

146

person who is loyal to other designated black people. But Hurston illustrates all too well how morally good American identities of mixed race collapse into black racial identities. Such black identities may be admirable, but they are not logically or in fact identities of mixed race.

III

THE PHILOSOPHY of ANTI-RACE

14

Nobility versus Good Faith

A colleague of mine who read Chapter 3, in which I discussed the work-in-life or existential uses of postscientific white racism, was nonplussed by what he called my parody of Martin Heidegger.[1] As an undergraduate and as a graduate student, I had a solemn philosophical respect for Heidegger. I still subscribe to the view that work or art is separable from the character or personality of its creator. So it was not my intention to make fun of Martin Heidegger in Chapter 3 or to attack his early philosophy because he was accused of collaborating with the Third Reich later on. Rather, I was looking for a philosophical context in which to make sense of postscientific white racism and the conceptual framework of Heidegger's *Being and Time* was ready-to-mind. Here was a profound explanation of the importance of the past and of the obligation to take up one's life as a negation, as well as a framework within which to relate to others on the basis of that negation. Then, later in Heidegger's thinking, there was a built-in nationalism or chauvinism when he insisted that the kind of primary philosophical thinking that interrogates Being could take place only in the German language.[2] This was not a privileging of modern German as opposed to modern French, English, or Italian—although Heidegger did refuse to allow his work to be translated into Spanish—but a privileging of the German language insofar as it led back to the ancient Greek language.[3]

After Heidegger turned against *humanism* in his *kehre*, he thought that *the* problem confronting contemporary humans was the problem of technology. This was technology as a technologizing, world historical force; technology as the tail that wags the dog of modern science; technology as the *enframing* tool which cannot be controlled by the sorcerer's apprentice and can destroy the whole world. It was technology as a force beyond human *being* which had the possible saving grace of alerting human beings to how they were alienated from *Being*.[4] Heidegger made it clear that this technology was European in general and German in particular. He thought that German thinkers such as himself had a special relation, through the deep etymology of the German language, to that cradle of European technology which was ancient Greece.[5]

Heidegger's etymological studies have been fiercely debated and perhaps even discredited, but that is of minor importance here. Whether or not German concepts concerning Being can be derived from untranslatable pre-Socratic ideas is not the issue, for this reason: Quite apart from Heideggarian linguistic studies, there is a strong belief throughout the history of Western culture that modern European science began with the speculations of the pre-Socratic philosophers. Not only is there this consensus about the origins of science as we know it, but modern European art, philosophy, and all of the important aspects of Western mental culture are held to have their foundation within ancient Greek culture, both before and after Socrates.

Furthermore, the issue of Greek foundationism leads directly into contemporary American disputes about which texts ought to be required reading in egalitarian higher education.[6] If the traditional canon is Eurocentric, so the argument goes, and Eurocentricity privileges the white race and white racisms, then the traditional canon has to be radically (racially?) modified. Almost everyone involved in this discussion traces the Eurocentric canon back to Plato and Aristotle, who both endorsed elitism, patriarchy, slavery and almost all else in that higher culture which is now perceived to exclude poor people, women, and non-whites.

According to Martin Bernal, the tradition of believing foundational Greek culture to be coextensive with the achievements of people who were racially white began in the nineteenth century. In *Black Athena*, Bernal makes an interesting scholarly case that the ancient Greeks themselves freely acknowledged a historical cultural debt to the racially non-white cultures of Asia and Africa.[7] If Bernal is correct, then the foundations of Western culture are as much Afrocentric as Eurocentric. Why is this important?

At the end of the last chapter, I reached a point where it became necessary to question the need for, or to seek a justification of, ethnic or racial identity as a present process of identification with individuals, events, or traditions in the past. I was not looking for an understanding of black or white racial identity but for an understanding of what would be involved in constructing an identity of mixed black and white race, based on the past. The search for this understanding privileges American individuals of mixed race because the strongly negative history of mixed race in the United States means that any positive mixed-race identity would have to be created almost from scratch. The privilege here lies in not having been handed a ready-made ethnic history but, instead, in being confronted with the monumental task of putting such an identity together, beginning now. This is the privilege of being free to choose the components of one's identity. And even more luxurious than that privilege is the freedom to ask this question: Why should a mixed-race person bother to do it? Obviously, European whites, and now blacks also, think that such projects are worthwhile. The whites have their roots in what they have believed for about 150 years to be white ancient Greek civilization. The blacks may be able to trump them with roots that are longer, or deeper, or older—it is not clear what the botanical metaphor entails.

The questions about an identity based on the past that a mixed-race American must confront begin with this person's alienation from the past. So in this breach it makes sense to ask: Why is *older* better? What is so important about the past as a source of identity?

There is no reason to assume that identification with the past makes people happier. If anything, it may impose obligations and restrictions that diminish chances for individual happiness. Neither can a rational case be made that individuals have an ethical obligation to the past—how can one have a debt or an answerability to people and situations that no longer exist? How can one be respon-

sible for events that took place before one was born? If the past
with which one identifies causes anger at people to whose living
descendants it is deemed appropriate to direct that anger, then the
past can become a motive for revenge. Revenge may impart drama
to life, but why would one want to seek revenge as a motive?[8]
Why should anyone take up the past as part of a project of self-
identity?

Friedrich Nietzsche offers an inadvertant answer to the last
question in his discussion of noble values in *Beyond Good and
Evil*: "It is the powerful who *know* how to honour, it is their art,
their domain for invention. The profound reverence for age and for
tradition—all law rests on this double reverence—the belief and
prejudice in favour of ancestors and unfavourable to newcomers, is
typical of the morality of the powerful."[9]

Nietzsche here assumes a relation between power and a reverence for tradition. This connection between an aristocracy and its
past, through its traditions, is part of the strength of noble groups,
and it points to the discipline that they had to impose on themselves in the past in order to become strong:

> A type with few, but very marked features, a species of severe,
> warlike, wisely silent, reserved and reticent men (and as such,
> with the most delicate sensibility for the charm and *nuances* of
> society) is thus established, unaffected by the vicissitudes of
> generations; the constant struggle with uniform *unfavourable*
> conditions is, as already remarked, the cause of a type becoming
> stable and hard.[10]

Other than a wish to become a powerful and predatory aristo-
crat, there could be more ordinary reasons for identifying with the
past, such as needs for communal pride and pleasant feelings about
the self. However, without the discipline required to become noble
and the noblesse oblige of a ruling elite, communal pride and self-
satisfaction could slide into chauvinism and selfishness, and nobility might be no more than compensatory delusion. That is how
Jean-Paul Sartre analyzes the French anti-Semite, for example.

It may seem farfetched to compare the possibilities of a positive American mixed-race identity with an identity that civilized
people everywhere now condemn. After all, as Jean-Paul Sartre

and R. M. Hare (among others) have pointed out, the anti-Semite cannot be reasoned with and his views cannot be rejected as mere matters of taste.[11] The racial identity of the anti-Semite is based on what he hates, and for this reason his racial identity is extremely suspect. But it is precisely because the racial identity of the anti-Semite is suspect, in a way which makes all well-intended people uncomfortable, that this identity might provide an instructive measure for a presumably value-positive identity of mixed race. It is still not a foregone conclusion that any ethnic or racial identity can be free of malevolent or unjust motives, i.e., free of hate. But to criticize the positive racial identity of a group whom all well-meaning people take to be an oppressed group—a group such as American blacks, for example—would be to add to the oppression and thereby taint the criticism. Therefore, because the French anti-Semite is a deserving target of criticism, I am now going to track Sartre's analysis of the French anti-Semite from the standpoint of an American of mixed black and white race. The aim of this exercise is to determine whether the construction of an American mixed-race identity, based on the past, would be a worthwhile project if it were possible. That is, would such a project clear the types of *bad faith* exemplified by the French anti-Semite?

There are five aspects of French anti-Semitic ethnicity, as addressed by Sartre, that are relevant to the project of a mixed-race racial identity: attachment to the past; choice of passion over reason; choice of immanence over freedom; communality that transcends social class; privileging one's own racial body. Sartre has analyzed these structures of anti-Semitism from the standpoint of how they determine Jewish identity and oblige Jews to be *authentic*. But his analysis of the structures of the anti-Semite's consciousness and experience outlines the core of a traditional ethnicity in ways that are not usually perceived to be connected with racism and hatred. The connections are clear in the case of the anti-Semite because his motives are already exposed. But as Sartre presents him, the French anti-Semite has constructed his identity in ways that are comparable to American white and American black racial identities.

However, no one has yet addressed the cores of American

[margin note: a — similar point made by Adrian Piper]

[margin note: ? really?]

black and white racial identities as Sartre has addressed the core of the anti-Semite's racial identity. When Americans analyze their own racial identities or those of what they take to be the opposing race, they usually do so in an ideological context that quickly becomes charged with the racisms and counterracisms that are being rhetorically addressed. Understandably, but regrettably, this rhetoric, which is ideology, precludes the possibility of theoretical inquiry—it is already too normative. But for an American of mixed black and white race to compare her possible racial identity to the anti-Semitism of a Frenchman does, I submit, have sufficient distance to allow for the possibility of open-minded inquiry. Let us then consider the relevant parts of Sartre's analysis, beginning in each instance with a key passage from *Anti-Semite and Jew*.

The Attachment to the Past

> The true Frenchman, rooted in his province, in his country, borne along by a tradition twenty centuries old, benefitting from ancestral wisdom, guided by tried custom, does not *need* intelligence. His virtue depends upon the assimilation of the qualities which the work of a hundred generations has lent to the objects which surround him.[12]

This attachment to the past is not available to an American of mixed race. All conservatives and traditionalists have to invent a valued past in the present and project this past onto the future. But they have some basic material to begin with: the recognition of themselves in ethnic terms, by others, as descendants of forebears like them; and the success of those forebears. An American of mixed race has no past identity on which to project herself and which she can project onto the future. Nevertheless, she is able to exist as well or better than those who do have these things. Her functioning in modern society is less impeded by nostalgia for older social structures, and she knows that all of the dislocations of contemporary life, from the ever new alienations of those with ethnic histories to the undermining of patriarchy, work in her favor. She has the asset of having always been dislocated and doubly alienated, while those new victims of change are floundering.

The classic philosophical problem with induction, as posed by

THE PHILOSOPHY OF ANTI-RACE

David Hume, is not merely that there is no logical guarantee that the future will resemble the past but that there is no connection between discrete events in time that is determined by anything that is an intrinsic part of those events. Thus the logical gap between cause and effect has the same structure as the gap between past and future. This twofold problem of induction is usually posed from the standpoint of an agent anticipating the future. But there is a reverse chronological problem of induction that is even more difficult: There is no glue that connects present reality with past reality or the who and what of an agent with the who and what of her ancestors. For someone who has not had an ethnic past handed to her through "a hundred generations," laying claim to the past seems to involve even more epistemological risk than predicting the future—especially because one has to use up some of one's uncertain future to construct a history. There is no certainty that the past was as one imagines it, no intrinsic connection between who one is now and who someone else was in the past. To forge a connection between the present and an imagined past would be somehow to cause one's own past, a project that would seem to require great leaps of epistemic faith.

The Choice of Passion over Reason

> The anti-Semite has chosen hate because hate is a faith; at the outset he has chosen to devaluate words and reasons. . . .
>
> If then, as we have been able to observe, the anti-Semite is impervious to reason and to experience, it is not because his conviction is strong. Rather his conviction is strong because he has chosen first of all to be impervious.[13]

No matter how unsatisfactory the universalism of liberals and the pretense of rational detachment by privileged people may be to a member of an oppressed group, the choice of passion over reason changes nothing in the external world in a situation of oppression. An American of mixed race will have reached a realization that she is of mixed race only through the use of reason. The choice of passion to ground a mixed-race identity is therefore an impossibility. Rather, the mixed-race American is condemned to something like Sartre's vision of the truth: "The rational man groans as he gropes for the truth; he knows that his reasoning is no more than tentative, that other considerations may supervene to cast doubt on it. He never sees very clearly where he is going; he is 'open'; he may even appear to be hesitant."[14]

The Choice of Immanence over Freedom

> Anti-Semitism is not merely the joy of hating; it brings positive pleasures too. By treating the Jew as an inferior and pernicious being, I affirm at the same time that I belong to the elite. This elite, in contrast to those of modern times which are based on merit or labor, closely resembles an aristocracy of birth. There is nothing I have to do to merit my superiority, and neither can I lose it. It is given once and for all. It is a *thing*.
>
> Now the anti-Semite flees responsibility as he flees his own consciousness, and choosing for his personality the permanence of rock, he chooses for his morality a scale of petrified values.[15]

Not having a racial identity to begin with, the American of mixed race would have to deliberately invent this kind of solidity as a basis for racial identity or as a racial identity. This creative activity of invention would underlie any pretense at immanence. The solidity or *thinghood* projected onto the self and the subsequent pretense that it has always been there would be too great a lie to conceal from the self, even if others were fooled. Knowledge of the immanence of race precludes a free choice of racial identity. If having a race means having an essence that confers on the self fixed being like that of animal specieness, furniture, or stones, then if someone values her transcendence she would be unable to choose the thinghood of race, regardless of the social benefits of a racial identity.

All oppressed ethnic groups build their identities in part on the basis of how they have suffered from oppression. Some of this suffering consists of their awareness of deprivation in comparison to the oppressing group and their exclusion from the oppressing group. This is the kind of suffering that is called "alienation." But the person of mixed black and white race suffers from an alienation from the suffering of black individuals, as well as from her alienation from white individuals insofar as she is identified as

THE PHILOSOPHY OF ANTI-RACE

black. Her alienation is thereby compounded, although her alienation from the suffering of black individuals, which is part of her
inability to form a black identity, may be a limiting case of alienation, the point at which alienation becomes freedom. If freedom is
a higher value than racial identity and the two are not compatible,
surely the person of mixed race will continue to choose freedom.
This means that anyone in the position of having to deliberately
construct a racial identity must remain *race-less*.

Communality versus Social Class

> All they have to do is nourish a vengeful anger against the rob-
> bers of Israel and they feel at once in possession of the entire
> country. True Frenchmen, good Frenchmen are all equal, for
> each of them possesses for himself alone France whole and indi-
> visible.[16]

According to Sartre, the anti-Semite lives in an imaginary
community that transcends modern class barriers, the restrictions
of modern law, and all social rewards based on labor and merit.
Even money and what is bought with money is scorned by the
anti-Semite, because he views money as the impersonal medium
through which Jewish conspiracies operate.[17]

An American of mixed black and white race could easily fall
into the same illusion of belonging to a community that is not part
of the way that things work in contemporary society. This community might be nothing less than the class of all people who are not
racially pure or racially identifiable in the way in which a biracial
system assumes that everyone is racially identifiable. The French
anti-Semite is a Manichaean. He believes that the primary project
of his life, which is of course a noble one, is to combat evil.[18] A
person of mixed race who believed in a racially impure community
as the true reality underlying the injustice of a biracial system
could fall into an analogous Manichaeism, in which it was believed that all of the evils of the world were the result of racial
categories.

Sartre emphasizes the anti-Semite's disrespect for law and authority. The French anti-Semite does not consider the government
of France to be a legitimate government; instead, it is held to be

the outward form of a conspiracy.[19] This kind of rebelliousness is a pitfall for anyone who identifies himself as a member of an oppressed group. An oppressed group is oppressed by the whole of society, and the government, as a part of society, will contribute to the oppression. Paradoxically, the oppression of a minority through the government may be a direct result of democratic principles that entail that the government must express the mores of the majority. But this does not mean that the government is any less legitimate or "real"; nor does it mean that changing the government or the laws will necessarily change society.

The rebelliousness of the French anti-Semite is one to which all malcontents are subject. It is no longer necessary for Americans of mixed black and white race to break the law in order to reject externally imposed, punitive racial identities. But the insistence on a distinct racial identity by a person of mixed race is a violation of mainstream mores and custom, just as his biological existence is evidence of the violation of sexual taboos by people in the past. However, unlike the French anti-Semite, who constructs and chooses his hatred, an American of mixed race is forced to rebel as soon as he becomes aware of the significance of his existence in a biracial system.

Sartre does not speak of the rebelliousness of Jews in the face of anti-Semitism, but the concept applies. Sartre thought that Jews had been brought into existence historically as a result of anti-Semitism. He criticized Jews who were in flight from this situation through their denial of the stereotypes projected onto them by anti-Semites. According to Sartre, many virtues of the *inauthentic* Jew were poisoned by the fact that in addition to having the virtues, the Jew found it necessary to will having them in order to disprove an anti-Semitic stereotype. For example, if a Jew were generous, the generosity would be robbed of its spontaneity if the Jew were aware of being generous as a contradiction of an anti-Semitic stereotype that portrayed Jews as stingy.[20]

Sartre's concept of authenticity for Jews involved not a rebellion against anti-Semitism, which resulted in inauthentic flight from being a Jew, but a rebellion against that liberal tolerance which accepted the Jew as an ahistorical, universal human—a

THE PHILOSOPHY OF ANTI-RACE

man—but rejected him as a Jew. Sartre's requirement for a free society was that all citizens accept pluralism and extend full rights and considerations to the members of all minority groups, not as abstract humans but as the minorities they are:

> What we propose here is a concrete liberalism. By that we mean that all persons who through their work collaborate toward the greatness of a country have the full right of citizens of that country. What gives them this right is not the possession of a problematical and abstract "human nature," but their active participation in the life of the society. This means, then, that the Jews—and likewise the Arabs and the Negroes—from the moment that they are participants in the national enterprise, have a right in that enterprise; they are citizens. But they have these rights *as* Jews, Negroes, or Arabs—that is, as concrete persons.[21]

Sartre was concerned that minorities not develop reactive identities as a result of their devaluation by their oppressors but that they first accept their impossible situations as oppressed groups. However, he felt that this acceptance was a moral matter only.[22] For social change to occur and for oppression to end, it would be necessary for the oppressors to exchange what they thought was tolerance for an acceptance of those groups that had been forced into existence by oppression. Presumably, after this kind of a *pluralistic* society had come about, there would be less need for all reactive ethnic identities—the requirement of "active participation in the life of the society" suggests universal standards. But members of minorities have not always agreed with this optimistic prognosis by Sartre. Franz Fanon, for example, felt that Sartre had devalued his uniquely black experience with this kind of optimism:

> The dialectic that brings necessity into the foundation of my freedom drives me out of myself. It shatters my unreflected position. Still in terms of consciousness, black consciousness is immanent in its own eyes. I am not a potentiality of something, I am wholly what I am. I do not have to look for the universal. No probability has any place inside me. My Negro consciousness does not hold itself out as a lack. It *is*. It is its own follower.
> . . . What is certain is that, at the very moment when I was trying to grasp my own being, Sartre, who remained The Other,

gave me a name and thus shattered my last illusion. . . .

. . . Without a Negro past, without a Negro future, it was impossible for me to live my Negrohood. Not yet white, no longer wholly black, I was damned. Jean-Paul Sartre had forgotten that the Negro suffers in his body quite differently from the white man.[3]

Whether or not Sartre did cherish the universalism which Fanon accuses him of—a universalism that will always be more comfortable to people of mixed race in a biracial system, because they cannot hand themselves Fanon's sort of immanence—it is certainly possible that Sartre believed that some degree of universalism could coexist with particular ethnic diversities. Sartre had a lifelong interest in the problems of French Jews. In his old age he befriended a young Jewish woman who was deeply troubled by the experiences of her family during World War II. He was very fond of this woman and committed himself to helping her. But his chosen method of assistance was a fairly traditional psychological approach: He wanted her to be more assertive and to remember events from her childhood; he advised her to see a psychiatrist.[24] This kind of psychological solution supports a universalist interpretation of Sartre's final position on ethnic problems.

The Privileging of One's Own Racial Body

For these latter [the French anti-Semites], the body is a fruit of the French soil; they possess it by that same profound and magical participation which assures them the enjoyment of their land and their culture. Because they are proud of it, they have attached to it a certain number of values that are strictly irrational but are intended to express the idea of *life* as such. Scheler has accurately called them "vital values"; in effect, they concern neither the elementary needs of the body nor the demands of the spirit, but a certain blossoming, a certain biological style that seems to be a manifestation of the intimate functioning of the organism, the harmony and independence of the organs, the cellular metabolism, and above all the "life plan," that blind and wily design which is the very essence of life. Grace, nobility, vivacity are among these values. In fact, we ascribe them even to animals: we speak of the grace of a cat, of the nobility of the eagle.[25]

The aesthetic purity of white bodies, the rhythm and elemental sexuality of black bodies, the exotic eroticism of mixed-race bodies and their fancied debilities—all of these fantastic illusions are a cornucopia of physical choices for a person of mixed race. And if one is a woman, there are additional fetishes and mysteries of gender to add to the array. Whether all or some of these magical physical qualities can be used to underpin a concept of special physical vitality, of life, that overrides normal biological life is beyond detached inquiry. An American of mixed race is more often than not afflicted with the fantasies of her body that others have constructed. Doubtless she is fortunate if she is as physically attractive as she wants to be and as physically healthy as she needs to be. Like anyone else, she is sane if she accepts her body, blessed if she likes it.

Some Americans of mixed black and white race might place a higher value on what they agree are the shared physical attributes of people of mixed race. In any case, it is difficult to see how such enjoyment of special traits is any worse (or any better) than the racial fantasies of blacks or whites about their own bodies. Vanity and physical self-absorption are not, on the face of it, harmful to others, as long as these projects are removed from the devaluation of other people's bodies racially.

The possibility of an American identity of mixed race is still open theoretically, even after looking at Sartre's analysis of an extreme case of ethnic identity. The world of power is at best indifferent to the racial identities of non-white minorities—although it is tireless in identifying them—so it would be mildly negative at best to identities of mixed race in a biracial system. An American of mixed race is unlikely to fall into any of the traps of racial identity that involve imbuing the self with fixed, thing-like qualities. These traps need external recognition and a shared history, neither of which is available to Americans of mixed race. Perhaps it is the very racelessness of being of mixed race in a biracial system that makes the possibility of such an identity valuable. It would have to be an identity that looks to the future rather than to the past, an identity founded on freedom and resistance to oppression rather than immanence and acceptance of tradition. If this is a "view from nowhere," the position of nobody, based on nothing, it is more authentic than projections of the self onto "one hundred generations" that bear no relation to the self in the dimension to which one might turn for self-identification as a human being. An American who identifies herself as mixed black and white race is a new person racially, because old racial categories do not allow her to identify herself this way. It is such a person's very newness racially that gives her the option of racelessness. To be raceless in contemporary racial and racist society is, in effect, to be *anti-race*. If 'authenticity' is a definition of the self in the face of oppression, then the authenticity of a person of mixed race may rest on her resistance to biracial racial categories—the racial authenticity of mixed race could therefore be the racial position of anti-race.

15

Black, White,
and Gray:
Words, Words, Words

I want to conclude this book on an emancipatory but possibly conciliatory note that avoids hypocrisy. I do not wish to betray the alienation of persons of mixed race in the biracial American system. It is not that such persons have "difficulty" with their black identities but that they cannot conclusively choose any one racial identity.[1] The emancipation I aim for is that form of universalism that lies on the other side of diversity. I have to call it "liberalism." By 'liberalism' I mean a goal of the maximum amount of benevolence toward the maximum number of people, which is compatible with the maximum amount of respect for individual freedom. These maxima are matters of intuition: Benevolence is an intuitive good; freedom is a subjective necessity; subjective necessities override maximum social goods because individuals are the final sentient recipients of all goods.

Individual freedom cannot be defined absolutely for all time. It is a continual process of peeling away the onion of coercion, and what is seen to be coercive today would have been unthinkable as coercive yesterday. For example, before the 1920s white Anglo-Saxon Americans believed that Italian, Irish, and Polish immigrants were distinct races.[2] No one would suggest that now. The concept of black American race has no uniform factual or moral foundation, and when people are identified as racially black, they do not get the same treatment as people who are identified as racially white. So perhaps the time has come to reject the concept of a black American race, because that concept is coercive.

As a symbol of emancipatory liberalism, my mind dwells on a

165

surprisingly obscure photograph. I came across the picture in a book about Pablo Picasso's life and work when I was taking a break from thinking about Chapter 3. An informally posed group of artists and writers stand in a semicircle and sit on the floor in Picasso's studio in March 1944. Picasso has read his play *Le Desire attrape par la queue*. Jean-Paul Sartre sits on the floor, his elbows resting on his knees and his ankles crossed; he is smoking a pipe and gazing owlishly off to his right. To Sartre's left, Albert Camus attends to a large standard poodle named "Kazbek," while Michael Leiris looks on. Picasso stands solidly behind Camus, his arms folded as he looks squarely at the camera. Between and behind Camus and Leiris stands Simone de Beauvoir. She is soberly dressed, with braids crowning her head, a book in her hands, and an old-fashioned reticule hanging from her arm. Others—Jacques Lacan, Cecile Eluard, Pierre Reverdy, Louise Leiris, Zanie Aubier, Jean Aubier, and Valentine Hugo—are also there.[3] But I was struck by the presence of Jean-Paul Sartre, Simone de Beauvoir, Michael Leiris, and Pablo Picasso in the same room toward the end of World War II. They were all strong liberals whose lives' works were based on themes of human freedom in ways that are meaningful to my own life and work.

The way in which Sartre analyzed anti-Semitism in the context of human freedom has been discussed in Chapter 14. Simone de Beauvoir's *The Second Sex*, first published in 1949, was a fundamental component of the second wave of feminism in the twentieth century.[4] Michael Leiris was head of research at the Centre National de la Recherche Scientifique and a staff member of the Musée de l'Homme in Paris during the 1950s.[5] His work on race and culture was an important contribution to the international destruction of the paradigm that held that cultural traits were physically inheritable. The following passage by Leiris characteristically states this shift from genetics to history as an explanatory source of *difference*:

> In our own day, the task of the anthropologist is to study cultures diverging considerably from what with certain variants is the common culture of the Western nations. This must suggest the question whether there is a causal relationship between race

and culture and whether each of the various ethnic groups has on balance a predisposition to develop certain cultural forms. However, such a notion cannot survive a scrutiny of the facts and it can be taken as established today that hereditary physical differences are negligible as causes of the differences in culture observable between the peoples. What should rather be taken into consideration is the history of those peoples.[6]

Although Picasso brought the horrors of the Spanish Civil War to mass cultural attention with his painting *Guernica*, art was probably more important to him than any political event or social situation.[7] Still, the lived autonomy of an artist always reinforces individual ideas about human freedom. Sartre, de Beauvoir, Leiris, and Picasso were all champions of human freedom—they were all liberals.

Richard Rorty says that a liberal is someone who will not accept cruelty: "I borrow my definition of 'liberal' from Judith Shklar, who says that liberals are the people who think that cruelty is the worst thing we do."[8] In this Shklar–Rorty sense, liberalism would be a species of utilitarianism, a public and political commitment to benevolence toward all. As Rorty is aware, a private sense of liberalism is also necessary for human freedom.[9] One should be as free from external restraints as possible in choosing who and what one is. A precise phenomenology of subjective freedom has yet to become a legitimate 'mainstream' philosophical subject. But I have been arguing throughout this work that in a context where a race is devalued, such as in the United States, racial designations are as racist, i.e., as cruel, as racist devaluations. Such racial designations limit individuals in their subjectivities, even when they take up the designations themselves, about themselves. The mythology about race which underlies racial devaluations and racial designations is evident in the language of race that is used in the United States. Everyone knows that racial epithets and slurs represent a breakdown of normal cooperative assumptions of communication—these derogatory *race-words* are insults and as such easily bridge gaps between words and action.[10] But people are less aware of the way in which seemingly neutral racial language is racist. Because the racism inherent in various concepts of race has aly been discussed, it seems appropriate at this point to turn to words themselves.

First, there is a general myopia about the black–white dichotomy. When Americans hear the word "race," they immediately assume it means "black" or "white." In many places, for long periods of time in American history, all people could be divided into black or white racial categories. This was before there were large numbers of Hispanic Americans, Asian Americans, and recognized Native Americans. It was before these other racial groups became large or strong enough to demand recognition or, as in the case of Native Americans, before they were permitted voices which could be heard by some of those in the society from which they had been alienated. The black–white racial dichotomy imposes a myopic linguistic convention, which holds that everyone belongs to a race but that there are only two races: Negro and Caucasian. Of course, even the most emphatic biracialists know that there are also Asians, but when the topic of race comes up they speak as if everyone were either black or white.

In Anglo-American cultural history, the words "black" and "white" are symbols with positive and negative moral connotations. Sin in the sense of sexual transgression, for example, is 'black,' and virginity and other traditional states of moral virtue are 'white.' Thus the black–white sin–virtue dichotomy was available historically as a justification for the exploitation of blacks by whites when Europeans first began to exploit Africa, the 'dark' continent.[11] (The moral-religious connotations of a black–white dichotomy are so exaggerated in American culture that it can be a locution of criticism, imputing ignorance, stupidity, and possibly insanity, to say that someone "sees" such and such "in black and white.")[12] In addition to this symbolism, there are other racist aspects of the American use of the black–white dichotomy of race.

There is no parity in the derivation of the words used for the two racial categories: Caucasian and Negro. The word "Caucasian" has a geographical reference to the Caucasus area and thereby derives from a proper name. The word "Negro" comes from the French or Spanish word *negro*, meaning the color black, which derives from the Latin word *niger*, having the same meaning.[13] Until the 1920s, American blacks were referred to as "negroes," with a small *n*. The insistence on the capital *N* was based on the demand for the acceptance of American blacks as a national group, like other national groups whose names were capitalized.[14] The insistence on the word "black" to refer to black Americans in the 1960s was, in this context, a change to an English translation of *negro*. When "black" is used to refer to black Americans as an ethnic group, it is capitalized. But when "black" is simply a racial designation in contrast to the racial designation "white," it is not capitalized. It is ironic that when American blacks insisted on racial respect, "Negro" became capitalized; and when Black Culture was revalued, "black" became the preferred racial designation. The word "white" as a racial designation is almost never capitalized these days, outside of white supremacist literature.

When American blacks are referred to as "African Americans," this appears to establish a parity of terminology with "Caucasian" because the word "African," like the word "Caucasian," is an adjective deriving from the proper name of a place. But people were first designated as Caucasian because of their resemblance to the physical appearance of people who inhabited the Caucasus geographical areas. By contrast, most American blacks are designated as African Americans on the basis of an assumption that they have forebears whose physical appearance resembled people who inhabit the geographical area of Africa. So again there is no parity.

The words "black" and "white" purport to categorize people racially on the basis of their skin color. There are some, but very few, Americans who have skin the actual colors of objects that are accurately described as having black and white surfaces. As colors, black and white are anomalous: In quasi-scientific language, black is the perceptual experience of the absence of all colors from the visible spectrum, and white is the perceptual experience of the presence of all colors from the visible spectrum.[15] (These optical facts make a joke out of the use of the sobriquet "of color" for all non-white people.) Still, it is possible to manufacture black and white pigments, and like all other colors that can be applied to the surfaces of objects, black and white can be mixed.

When the colors black and white are mixed, they produce various shades of gray. When people who are black and white "mix" genetically, it is commonly acknowledged that the skin colors of their offspring fall on a continuum of colors that are in the ranges of brown and tan. On one end of this continuum are those whose skin color would be called "white," in the absence of knowledge of their black forebears. On the other end of the continuum are those whose skin color would cause them to be racially designated black. Thus, as racial words, "black" and "white" purport to refer to skin color, but in fact they are only loosely related to the actual skin colors of human beings. In the case of individuals who are called "white" racially, the word "white" is not expected to refer either to their actual skin color or to the actual skin color of their ancestors. In the case of individuals who are called "black" racially, the word "black" may be believed to be a more accurate description of the skin color of their ancestors than of the individuals themselves.

By contrast, as Carl N. Degler describes the racial system in Brazil, there race is not determined by the race of a person's ancestors but by money. Thus a poor Brazilian mulatto is a Negro, whereas a rich Negro who is not visibly of mixed race is white. This has been called the "lightening" effect of money—and social class. American slave owners bred their slaves as a way of increasing their capital. This was less so in Brazil.[16] It may be that the strong hereditary aspect of American race derives from the strong property interest in the hereditary aspects of American slavery.[17] If this is so, it would suggest that Americans have stronger property traditions than Brazilians do. Even though Brazilians are now more "materialistic" about race, historically, Americans have been more materialistic about people, a form of materialism that lives on in all biracial American racial designations to this day (see Chapter 6).

There is every reason to believe that Americans are just as sentient of colors as people who live in other countries. That is, only a small percentage of Americans are color blind, or perceive only black, white, and gray. So it is fairly clear that the racial words "black" and "white" are not the color words that they purport to be but labels that refer to nineteenth-century concepts of race, which associated nonphysical characteristics with racial designations.

The current scientific view of a race is that a race is a group of people who have more of some physical traits than do other groups of people. Skin color is not a particularly accurate standard for determining races, nor is skin color in combination with body types, facial features, hair textures, or any of the other physical characteristics associated with races. Henry Louis Gates, Jr., makes the point of how inadequate those physical criteria are that purport to be racial criteria, in a quote from a contemporary American work on "Left" political theory:

> The division of the human species into races is biologically—though not socially—arbitrary. We could differentiate humans along countless axes, such as height, weight and other physical features. If we assigned racial categories to groups of humans with different heights—for example, every foot of height from four feet up determines a new race—we would be more biologically precise than the usual racial designation by skin color. For no fixed biological boundary exists between Asian and Caucasian, black and Indian, whereas a fixed boundary does exist between those who are shorter than five feet and those who are between five and six feet.[18]

However, it is not racial-group membership that determines race in the United States but lines of descent—genealogy. As groups, races are not stable entities. In Melville J. Herskovits's often-quoted words, "Two human groups never meet but they mingle their blood." And of course, this has always been the case in the United States. But due to the alchemy of American racism, no new race ever results. Black and white do not make gray here, but black.

It is important to note that when the acknowledgment of a mixed-race individual does not go beyond a reference to the racial diversity of that individual's forebears, the individual is called "of mixed race." But if the individual is acknowledged to be a racial mixture *in himself*, then he would be called "mixed race," without the "of." The use of the word "of" in the designation "of mixed race" leaves open the question of what the mixed-race individual *is* racially, and this "of" is compatible with the American one-drop rule. But if "of" is left out and an individual is called simply "mixed race," it becomes more difficult conceptually to designate that individual black (or white, for that matter).

It is interesting, however, that wherever there is some recognition that mixed-race people exist, as there was in the old lower South and as there still is in Brazil, the metaphors "black" and "white" are abandoned in favor of color words which come closer to describing what it is that people see when they look at skin colors.[19] The skin colors of people of acknowledged mixed race are called words such as "coffee," "almond," "almond shell," "piney," "honey," "ivory," "mahogany," "tan," and so on.[20] It is almost as if, in the presence of those individuals who are perceived to be mixed black and white race, the reality of human perception reasserts itself, and an attempt is made to speak the truth about visual experience. As offensive as such mixed-race color words may be against the backdrop of a biracial system, they nevertheless have more human reality than those color words "black" and "white" (which most Americans could never approximate in appearance without being badly burned or suffering massive blood loss).

However, once an American begins to formulate a theoretical entitlement to consideration as a mixed-race person, the word "gray" might look attractive as a racial name, for the sake of parity (even though it is now used to describe an appearance of illness in practically everyone, without prejudice). Of course, it would be a more liberal society if all people could be described physically as other natural objects are described (without anachronistic metaphors that, if taken literally, refer to death and disease). It would be a far more liberal society if racial designations were *allowed* to go the inevitable way of all historically vestigial categories. And if there is an intention that this be so, in the interim between the world of today, when people are categorized like so many breeds of domestic animals, and tomorrow, when the dog show will be over, what should "black," "non-white," "gray," and perhaps "red" and "yellow" people be called? Call us what we are, plain and simple: "racially designated."

THE PHILOSOPHY OF ANTI-RACE

NOTES,
BIBLIOGRAPHY,
INDEX

Notes

Preface

1. The paper was published as "An Autobiographical View of Mixed-Race and Deracination" in the *American Philosophical Association Newsletter on Philosophy and the Black Experience* 91, no. 1 (Spring 1992): 6–10.

2. For the statistics, see Lucius Outlaw, "From the Committee [on Blacks in Philosophy]," *Newsletter on Philosophy and the Black Experience* 90, no. 2 (Fall 1991): 10.

Chapter 2

1. The schema as I present it formalizes those concepts of race which are accepted by most writers in the black emancipatory tradition, as well as by both racist and "egalitarian" whites. See, for example, Anthony Appiah's apparent assumptions in "'But Would That Still Be Me?': Notes on Gender, 'Race,' Ethnicity as Sources of Identity," *Journal of Philosophy* 77, no. 10 (Oct. 1990): 493–99. Appiah is aware that the entire concept of race is a matter of culture, but he still accepts the concept (on that basis). My claim is that within our culture we use a physical concept of race, and it is this concept that needs to be addressed philosophically.

I thank Lawrence Ashley for pointing out (during a paper I gave at the Department of Philosophy at SUNY, Cortland) that my schema is a model rather than a description of cultural practices, with his question of how to determine the variables when cousins become parents (in that case, the grandparents-in-common would be counted twice).

2. This was not always the case in the United States. Between 1850 and 1915, white America moved from overlooking "some blackness in a person" to classifying persons with "one iota of color" as black. See

Willard B. Gatewood, *Aristocrats of Color* (Bloomington and Indianapolis: Indiana University Press, 1990): 149–51.

3. See, e.g., Robert C. Solomon, *Introducing Philosophy* (New York: Harcourt Brace Jovanovich, 1986), pp. 373 and 393. In discussing personal identity, Solomon assumes that racial designations are facts about the individuals so designated.

4. See, e.g., E. Ellis Cashmore and Barry Troyman, *Introduction to Race Relations* (London: Routledge & Kegan Paul, 1983), pp. 19–20.

5. See, e.g., Cashmore and Troyman, *Race Relations*, pp. 21–35; John Rex, *Race and Ethnicity* (Storey Stratford, England: Open University Press, 1986), pp. 1–37; Michael Leiris, "Race and Culture," in Leo Kuper, ed., *Race, Science and Society* (New York: Columbia University Press, 1965), pp. 135–72.

6. See, e.g., Max Gluckman, "New Dimensions of Change, Conflict and Settlement," in Kuper, ed., *Race, Science and Society*, pp. 320–39.

7. L. C. Dunn and Theodosius Dobzhansky, *Heredity, Race and Society* (New York: Mentor, 1960), pp. 114 and passim.

8. See, e.g., Dunn and Dobzhansky, *Heredity, Race and Society*, pp. 40–63; and L. C. Dunn, "Race and Biology," in Kuper, ed., *Race, Science and Society*, pp. 61–67.

9. For contemporary theories of blood groups and the genetics involved, see N. P. Dubinin, "Race and Contemporary Genetics," in Kuper, ed., *Race, Science and Society*, pp. 68–94.

10. See Otto Klineberg, "Race and Psychology," in Kuper, ed., *Race, Science and Society*, pp. 173–207.

11. See Dubinin, "Race and Contemporary Genetics," pp. 68–83, and idem, "Four Statements on the Race Question," originally published by UNESCO in 1950, 1951, 1964, 1967; reprint in Kuper, ed., *Race, Science and Society*, Appendix.

12. Ibid.

13. Ibid.

14. See W.E.B. Du Bois, "The Concept of Race" and "The White World," in idem, *The Dusk of Dawn: An Essay toward an Autobiography of a Race Concept*, reprinted in idem, *Du Bois Writings*, comp. Nathan Huggins, 1940; (reprint, New York: Literary Classics of the U.S., 1986), pp. 549–651, 665–66.

15. Ibid., p. 666. It is interesting that it is Du Bois, not the white racist, who takes up the identification of an individual racially, based on how that individual is treated, as if to acknowledge that his definition of race is no more based on scientific facts than that of the racist but is taken

up as a necessary reaction to what we would call "racism" today. Indeed, this was an insistent theme of Du Bois's throughout *Dusk of Dawn* and in his essays in *The Crisis* (1910–1934).

16. Leo Kuper, for example, in introducing his anthologized readings, which establish that cultural traits are not genetic, speaks of a "defense against racism" because "the arena of confrontation is essentially defined by racists" (*Race, Science and Society*, p. 14).

Chapter 3

1. Willard B. Gatewood, *Aristocrats of Color* (Bloomington and Indianapolis: Indiana University Press, 1990), p. 149; and L. C. Dunn, "Race and Biology," in Leo Kuper, ed., *Race, Science and Society* (New York: Columbia University Press, 1965), p. 31.

2. *Webster's New International Dictionary*, 2d ed., s.v. "race"; and *Encyclopaedia Britannica*, 11th ed., s.v. "race."

3. See, e.g., Daniel J. Kevles, *In the Name of Eugenics* (Berkeley: University of California Press, 1985), esp. chaps. on Francis Galton, Karl Peatson, and Charles Devenport, pp. 3–57.

4. For a recent dispute among contemporary professional philosophers about the importance of IQ and its black–white racial distribution, see the shameful claims made by Michael Levin and responses to them in "Letters to the Editor," *APA Proceedings and Addresses* 62, no. 6 (Jan. 1990), and 63, no. 7 (June 1990), respectively. See also Kevles, *Name of Eugenics*, p. 269 and passim.

5. M. I. Finley, *Ancient Slavery and Modern Ideology* (New York: Pelican, 1983), pp. 97, 117–19.

6. For a discussion of the overlap between racial and caste designations in Indian culture, see Andre Beteille, "Race, Caste and Ethnic Identity," in Kuper, ed., *Race, Science and Society*, pp. 211–34; for the development of views of the Manchus as a race in China, see Pamela Kyle Crossley, *Orphan Warriors* (Princeton: Princeton University Press, 1990); for a world survey of the problems of different minorities, see Georgina Ashworth, ed., *World Minorities*, 3 vols. (Sunberry, England: Quartermaine, 1977, 1978, 1980).

7. I read Du Bois as defining the black race problematically, as a necessary reaction to white racism. For example, he does not merely connect the twentieth century problems of Negroes and whites to the situation of Negroes after the Civil War, as a historical analysis, but he continually urges that Negroes find their identity in reactions to oppres-

sion. See W.E.B. Du Bois, *The Souls of Black Folk*, reprinted in John Hope Franklin, ed., *Three Negro Classics* (New York: Avon, 1965), pp. 209–39. In *Anti-Semite and Jew*, Jean-Paul Sartre makes the same demand of Jewish authenticity (see Chapter 14).

8. See, e.g., James C. Breeden, ed., *Advice to Masters: The Ideal in Slave Management in the Old South* (Westport, Conn.: Greenwood, 1980), esp. pp. 163–224, which purport to describe physiological differences between slaves and whites.

9. See my section "Breeding," Chapter 4.

10. The Negro upper class, whose members were often light-skinned and who were therefore called "Blue Veiners," was frequently accused of deliberate attempts to distance itself from the uneducated and less refined Negroes. The mass Negro press also accused this upper class of outright discrimination against darker-skinned Negroes. See Gatewood, *Aristocrats of Color*, p. 154 and passim; see also W.E.B. Du Bois, "The Colored World Within," in idem, *Dusk of Dawn*, reprinted in *Du Bois Writings*, comp. Nathan Huggins (1940; reprint, New York: Literary Classics of the U.S., 1986), pp. 681–715.

11. See, e.g., James Weldon Johnson, *The Autobiography of an Ex-Colored Man*, reprinted in Franklin, ed., *Three Negro Classics*. For Du Bois's use of the phase "the worst," see *Souls of Black Folk*, in Franklin, ed., *Three Negro Classics*, pp. 322–23.

12. Cf. David Theo Goldberg, ed., *Anatomy of Racism* (Minneapolis: University of Minnesota Press, 1990), pp. ix–xiv.

13. Ibid., p. xiv. As Goldberg puts it, "One primary undertaking is to rectify the widespread presumption that racism is (inherently) a set of irrational processes."

14. See James Ridgeway, *Blood in the Face* (New York: Thundermouth, 1990), p. 27.

15. For example, the Christian Identity followers believe that Anglo-Saxons were the real lost tribe of Israel. They think that Jews, blacks, and others of color were sent to earth as a scourge by God, and that after the Apocalypse, the earth will be rid of all these "mud people." See ibid., p. 17.

16. Ibid. See esp. the sections on David Duke's legitimate political efforts, pp. 145–47 and passim.

17. As one of John Langston Gwaltney's subjects, Curtis Thorton, puts it, "I understand why they [white people] don't want us to think they are prejudiced. But if most of them were not prejudiced, it wouldn't be a

prejudiced country" (John Langston Gwaltney, *Drylongso* [New York: Random House, 1980], p. xxix).

18. See Kwame Anthony Appiah, "Racisms," in Goldberg, ed., *Anatomy of Racism*, pp. 5–6.

19. Martin Heidegger, *Being and Time*, trans. John MacQuarrie and Edward Robinson (New York: Harper & Row, 1962), pp. 13–67. Obviously, 'instantiation' does not reflect a deep interpretation of Heidegger, but I know of no other succinct way to refer to the relation of the ontic to the ontological.

20. See Gunther Neske and Emil Kettering, eds., *Martin Heidegger and National Socialism* (New York: Paragon, 1990), p. xx; Martin Heidegger, "The Rectoral Address," in Neske and Kettering, ed., *Heidegger and National Socialism*, pp. 5–15.

21. Richard Rorty, *Contingency, Irony and Solidarity* (Cambridge: Cambridge University Press, 1988), pp. 13–20 and 106–20 and passim.

22. See Gwaltney, *Drylongso*, p. 85.

23. Cf. John H. Bracey, who says it is fallacious "to assume the existence of a nation state [is] a permanent truth for all time" (John H. Bracey, "The Black Middle Class: Help or Hindrance," in Mary C. Lynn and Benjamin D. Berry, eds., *The Black Middle Class: Proceedings of a Conference at Skidmore College* [Saratoga Springs, N.Y.: Skidmore College, 1980], pp. 52–53).

24. Neske and Kettering, eds., *Heidegger and National Socialism*, pp. 44–57, 61–89.

25. Ibid., p. 61; for Hannah Arendt's discussion of the term 'woodpath,' see Hannah Arendt, "For Martin Heidegger's Eightieth Birthday," in Neske and Kettering, eds., *Heidegger and National Socialism*, p. 210.

26. Martin Heidegger, *The Question Concerning Technology*, trans. William Lovitt (New York: Harper Torchbooks, 1977), pp. 3–35.

27. See Ridgeway, *Blood in the Face*, pp. 13–17.

28. Martin Heidegger, "The Television Interview," in Neske and Kettering, eds., *Heidegger and National Socialism*, p. 84.

29. The italic terms are from Heidegger's terminology in *Being and Time*.

30. Hans Jonas, "Heidegger's Resoluteness and Resolve," in Neske and Kettering, eds., *Heidegger and National Socialism*, pp. 197–203.

31. Ridgeway, *Blood in the Face*, p. 16.

32. See n. 29, above.

Chapter 4

1. The poverty of American black families as compared to American white families is so traditional that the dissemination of and consumption of these statistics is in itself probably part of institutionalized racism.

2. For a compact summary of the importance of the family as a social unit in the Western state, from ancient Athens to contemporary America, with regrets about the current decay in family morality and the ideals of liberal democracy, see Frederick D. Wilhelmsen, "The Family as the Basis for Political Existence," *Intercollegiate Review* 26, no. 2 (Spring 1991): 9–17.

3. W.E.B. Du Bois, ed., *Negro American Family* (New York: Negro University Press, 1969), p. 25.

4. See N. P. Dubinin, "Race and Contemporary Genetics," in Leo Kuper, ed., *Race, Science and Society* (New York: Columbia University Press, 1965), p. 84.

5. Ibid.

6. See Willard B. Gatewood, *Aristocrats of Color* (Bloomington and Indianapolis: Indiana University Press, 1990), p. 169.

7. See John Langston Gwaltney, *Drylongso* (New York: Random House, 1980), pp. xv–xvi, 73–91, 206–19; for a statement by Louis Farrakhan that Semitic Jews are not white whereas Ashkenazi Jews are, see "Interview in *National Alliances Newspaper*," in William Pleasant, ed., *Independent Black Leadership in America* (New York: Castillo International Publications, 1990), p. 43.

8. See Gwaltney, *Drylongso*, pp. 27–73, 114–21, and passim.

9. For example, here is how Eldridge Cleaver describes the racial theory of the black Muslim separatist Elijah Mohammad: The people of the earth were all original blacks sixty-three hundred years ago. Yacub, a mad black scientist on the isle of Patmos, bred whites out of a black population by a system of birth control that eliminated people of color in each generation. This process took hundreds of years to complete, but Yacub's final creation was "the white devil with the blue eyes of death." According to Cleaver when he wrote *Soul on Ice*, "Yacub's History" is an inversion of the miscegenation among black Americans caused by the sexual exploitation of black women by white men. It is interesting that as incisive as Cleaver was in this book about issues of racism and black and white gender, he failed to question the basic concepts of physical race. See Eldridge Cleaver, *Soul on Ice* (New York: Dell, 1968), p. 99.

10. See Gwaltney, *Drylongso*, pp. 179–206.

11. See ibid., pp. 194–200; see Wade W. Nobles and Lawford L. Goddard, *Understanding the Black Family* (Oakland, Calif.: The Institute for the Advanced Study of Black Family Life and Culture, 1984), p. 85.

12. See Gwaltney ref. in n. 7, above.

13. See Gwaltney, *Drylongso*, pp. 85–86.

14. Wilhelm Reich, *Character Analysis: The Function of the Orgasm* (New York: Farrar, Straus & Giroux, 1958).

15. See Cleaver, *Soul on Ice*, pp. 145–62, 188–92, and passim (for example).

16. See E. Franklin Frazier, *The Negro Family in the United States* (Chicago: University of Chicago Press, 1973), p. 369.

Chapter 5

1. See Wilhelm Reich, *The Mass Psychology of Fascism* (New York: Farrar, Straus & Giroux, 1970), pp. 34–98. Reich's main point is that such state-induced nostalgia in the hearts of the masses creates longings through which suppressed sexual energy can be channeled and mobilized by the state. Regardless of the truth of Reich's claim, it is interesting in the context of American society that family values are presumed to have been more strongly instantiated at some time in the past. Family values may have been stronger in the past, but the question is why nostalgia is effectively evoked in association with family values rather than, for instance, hopes for a future with social conditions that may never have existed before. Perhaps this attachment to the past is merely the emotive force behind conservatism.

2. See, for example, the traditional point of view expressed by Christina Sommers ("Philosophers against the Family," in Christina Sommers and Fred Sommers, ed., *Vice and Virtue in Everyday Life* [New York: Harcourt Brace Jovanovich, 1989], pp. 728–53) in a critique of what she views as the devaluation of family obligations by moral theorists in mainstream philosophy and by feminists who favor women's autonomy.

In fact, the feminist tradition has always shown respect for the family: Mary Wollstonecraft argued for the rights of women at least in part so that they could become better wives and mothers; John Stuart Mill echoed this argument of Wollstonecraft's; Betty Friedan (in *The Second Stage*) called for social changes to accommodate women's abiding commitment to family, as well as to career; and contemporary scholarly feminists construct ethics of caring and models of self-identity as loci of family relations, as do less theoretical Women's Studies scholars who emphasize the endurance of family responsibilities and commitments in the lives of working-class and non-white women.

3. Linda Nicholson analyzes the distinction between familial and political (or private and public) spheres as a historically contingent distinction that shaped theoretical aspects of both modern liberalism and Marxism (see Linda Nicholson, *Gender and History* [New York: Columbia University Press, 1986]). It follows from Nicholson's primary analysis that not only has the family changed in history, but there is no way to clearly refer to the family independently of some specific historical context. And not only is the form of the family always historically contingent, but references to past family forms are as well. Thus it would be naive to assume that families in the past exhibited a greater or more intense amount of those family values that have come to be values based on contemporary American family structures, simply because it is believed that those contemporary values would have been more easily expressed in past forms of the family. For example, it may be correct, as Christina Sommers claims, that contemporary institutional living arrangements for the elderly lack the kindness that would come from more personal and individualized care of the elderly. But it does not follow from this, as Sommers assumes, that when the elderly were all cared for in families, they were treated with such kindness and individualized concern. All that we know is that in the present social context, some institutionalized elderly are not having their basic social needs met, and that this lack does not express *present* family values. See Christina Sommers, "Where Have All the Good Deeds Gone?" in Sommers and Sommers, eds., *Vice and Virtue*, pp. 577–82.

4. See Lucius Outlaw's discussion of the black emancipatory tradition's position that the classical Marxist analysis, based on the primacy of the concept of class, does not adequately explain the experiences of twentieth century black Americans ("Towards a Critical Theory of 'Race,'" in David Theo Goldberg, ed., *Anatomy of Racism* [Minneapolis: University of Minnesota Press, 1990], pp. 58–83 and esp. 73–75). Outlaw notes the externally caused discontinuities in the black critical tradition but insists on the inadequacies of a Marxist analysis of American race, even though the concept of physical race is not scientific.

I am trying to show that it is the ordinary concept of physical race that expresses the kinds of racism that cut across class lines. That this concept is not scientific but is nonetheless adhered to by otherwise nonracists requires an explanation, which I have tried to construct in terms of the logic of American breeding mores and their relation to white family identity.

5. See, e.g., Barbara Christian's discussion of the black middle-class status of Alice Walker's characters in *The Color Purple*, even though the circumstances of those characters would not equal middle-class status if they were white ("What Celie Knows That You Should Know," in Goldberg, ed., *Anatomy of Racism*, pp. 135–46).

6. For an Afrocentric critique of American social science as applied to black families, see Wade W. Nobles and Lawford L. Goddard, *Understanding the Black Family* (Oakland: The Institute for the Advanced Study of Black Family Life and Culture, 1984). For political arguments that the problems within black American families are the result of white racism, see Lenora Fulani, "Fulani," in *Independent Black Leadership in America*, with an introduction by William Pleasant (New York: Castillo International Publications, 1990), pp. 54–89. For moral arguments in favor of traditional black families within racist environments that hold such families under siege, see Nathan Hare and Julia Hare, *The Endangered Black Family* (San Francisco: Black Think Tank, 1984).

7. Nicholson, *Gender and History*, pp. 105–33.

8. Ibid., p. 112. Nicholson cites Joan Loues Flandren (*Families in Former Times*, trans. Richard Southern [Cambridge: Cambridge University Press, 1974], p. 9) in assigning the origin of the contemporary form and concept of the family to the nineteenth century.

9. See, e.g., Hare and Hare, *Endangered Black Family*; and E. Franklin Frazier's moralizing tone in *The Negro Family in the United States* (Chicago: University of Chicago Press, 1973), pp. 3–50 and 209–95.

10. In a recent annotated bibliography of 722 books, articles, and dissertations about the black American family, almost every topic, from abortion to research, is approached with the hypothesis that common beliefs and previous scientific studies have been ethnocentric in favor of white families, with a resulting devaluation of black families. And it is the summarized conclusion of many of these studies that once the prejudiced assumptions are brought to the surface, new data contradict previous studies based on the prejudiced assumptions. See Lenwood G. Davis, comp., *The Black Family in the United States* (New York: Greenwood, 1986).

11. W.E.B. Du Bois, ed., *The Negro American Family* (New York: Negro University Press, 1969), p. 31; see pp. 42–80 for pictures of "Negro homes."

12. Ibid., pp. 18–26.

13. See, e.g., William S. McFeely's biography *Frederick Douglas's* (New York: Norton, 1991); and Anne Rice's novel about the free *gens de couleur* in antebellum New Orleans, *The Feast of All Saints* (New York: Random House, 1986). It seems safe to assume that if there were strong family ties between blacks and whites while slavery was in effect, such ties must continue to be at least as prevalent in the absence of the barrier and stigma of slavery.

Chapter 6

1. See Annette Baier, "A Naturalistic View of Persons," *APA Proceedings and Addresses* 65, no. 3 (Nov. 1991): 5–17.

2. Susan Bordo, *The Flight to Objectivity* (Albany: State University of New York Press, 1987), essay 6; Genevieve Lloyd, "The Man of Reason," in Ann Garry and Marilyn Pearsall, eds., *Women, Knowledge and Reality* (Boston: Unwin Hyman, 1989), pp. 111–24.

3. Patricia Hill Collins, "Implications of Black Feminist Perspectives in Research and Teaching" (Keynote Address, Conference on Integrating Class, Race, and Gender into the Curriculum and Research, SUNY at Albany, June 7, 1991).

4. Patricia J. Williams, *The Alchemy of Race and Rights* (Cambridge: Harvard University Press, 1991), pp. 50, 102, 121 and passim.

5. For example, Linda Nicholson referred to a grid in which race intersects with biological sex to form gender in "Theorizing Difference: The Problem of Biological Foundationism" (paper delivered at the Conference on Integrating Class, Race, and Gender into the Curriculum and Research, SUNY at Albany, June 8, 1991).

6. For an analytic development of an informed "view from nowhere," there is Thomas Nagel, *The View from Nowhere* (New York: Oxford University Press, 1986), esp. chaps. 4 and 9.

7. There are forms of genealogy and family history other than linear descent. Claude Lévi-Strauss, for example, refers to the elaborate kinship systems of the Australian aborigines, which are not limited to direct descent genealogies ("Race and History," in Leo Kuper, ed., *Race, Science and Society* [New York: Columbia University Press, 1965], pp. 114–15).

Within English culture, there are both ecclesiastical and legal systems for establishing the heirs of foundations (usually colleges) through collateral consanguinity of kin, i.e., relatives who share common ancestors but have different intervening forebears. See G. D. Squibb, *Founders' Kin* (Oxford: Oxford University Press, 1972).

8. I am speaking of history in a simple, positivistic sense in this context, a sense that J. A. Passmore (for example) makes clear in "The Objectivity of History," in Stuart Brown, John Fauvel, and Ruth Finnegan, eds., *Conceptions of Inquiry* (New York: Metheun, 1981), pp. 278–94.

9. See, e.g., Henry Odera Oruka, "Sagacity in African Philosophy," in Tsenay Serequeberhan, ed., *African Philosophy* (New York: Paragon, 1991), pp. 59–60.

10. See Squibb, *Founders' Kin*, p. 72; and Angus Baxter, *In Search of Your Roots* (Toronto: Macmillan, 1972), p. 275. Baxter notes that the Mormons believe that husbands, wives, and children are "sealed together" as family units for all eternity. Accurate genealogical information is necessary before "sealing" ceremonies can be performed in temples.

11. See, e.g., Elizabeth Stone, *Black Sheep and Kissing Cousins* (New York: Penguin, 1989), pp. 3–11.

12. See ibid., pp. 19–24; and Baxter, *Your Roots*, p. 5.

13. For example, for figures on black poverty, illegitimacy, and life expectancy in the recent past, see *The World Almanac* (New York: Pharos Books, 1991), pp. 561, 836, 852. For older tables, see W.E.B. Du Bois, ed., *Negro American Family* (New York: Negro University Press, 1969); and E. Franklin Frazier, *The Negro Family in the United States* (Chicago: University of Chicago Press, 1973), indexes and tables. For a citation of recent crime statistics, see Williams, *Race and Rights*, pp. 73–74, 75, 77.

14. Indians were also enslaved in the New World, and both Indians and poor whites were enslaved in early colonial times. But by 1781 the only American slaves were black. See Oliver C. Cox, *Caste, Class and Race* (New York: Doubleday, 1959), pp. 324, 338; Derrick Bell, *And We Are Not Saved* (New York: Basic Books, 1987), pp. 38–42.

15. This is, I think, a general fact of American life. As one of Anne Rice's characters puts it in *The Feast of All Saints* (New York, Random House, 1986), "There is not one of us, . . . not one of us who is not descended from a slave! To my knowledge no coterie of African aristocrats ever settled willingly on these shores!" (p. 277).

16. Many of those who did win freedom had to buy their spouses and children from their former owners. And some of the former slaves who purchased their own wives did not free them. See Frazier, *Negro Family*, p. 139.

17. See Williams, *Race and Rights*, pp. 156–58.

18. Actually, the question of whether the child of slaves is born a slave seems never to have been a serious issue anywhere; although, as will be evident in the next chapter, in the United States at least there was controversy over whether the child of a slave and a free person should be a slave. On the issue of the greater ease of manumission without enduring stigma in the ancient world, as compared to the United States, see M. I. Finley, *Ancient Slavery and Modern Ideology* (New York: Pelican, 1983), pp. 75–76; and Thomas Wiedemann, *Greek and Roman Slavery* (Baltimore: Johns Hopkins University Press, 1981), pp. 25–26, 244–45.

19. John Locke, *Second Treatise on Government*, ed. William S. Carpenter (London: J. M. Dent & Sons, 1989), p. 210.

20. Ibid., sec. 85, p. 158.

21. Ibid., secs. 123, 124, pp. 179–80.

22. Thus, according to Locke, since man is not the author of his own life, he has no right to commit suicide and cannot voluntarily give that life over to another (Locke, *Second Treatise*, sec. 23, p. 128).

23. See Bell, *We Are Not Saved*, pp. 13–51, for the property and political reasons, based on southern property interests, for accommodating slavery at the Constitutional Convention in 1787; and see p. 34 for the specific constitutional citations, as originally listed by William Wiecek.

24. In 1967 the U.S. Supreme Court effectively struck down the antimiscegenation laws on the books in sixteen states. See Benjamin Muse, *The American Negro Revolution* (Bloomington: Indiana University Press, 1968), p. 280.

25. Williams, *Race and Rights*, p. 207.

26. Ibid., p. 228.

27. Ibid., p. 234.

28. Ibid., p. 236.

29. Ibid., pp. 154–55.

30. Ibid., pp. 110–15.

Chapter 7

1. Joel Williamson, *New People* (New York: Free Press, 1980), pp. xi–xii.

2. Cf. David Theo Goldberg, "The Social Formation of Racist Discourse," in idem, ed., *Anatomy of Racism* (Minneapolis: University of Minnesota Press, 1990), pp. 295–318.

3. It might seem odd to refer to an anthropologist and not to a sociologist. Traditionally, anthropologists study exotic and non-white cultures and sociologists study American and European cultures. This distinction captures the distancing (and *differencing*) inherent in anthropology and not in sociology. Sociologists may accept words and concepts uncritically because they come from the sociologists' own culture. Anthropologists are more likely to base their inquiries on the assumption that they are studying what to them are exotic and unusual cultural phenomena, which need to be explained, and that is the kind of critical light that needs to be turned onto American racial words and categories.

4. Henry Odera Oruka, "Sagacity in African Philosophy," in Tsenay Serequeberhan, ed., *African Philosophy* (New York: Paragon, 1991), pp. 49–52.

5. Ibid.

6. See L. C. Dunn and Theodosius Dobzhansky, *Heredity, Race and Society* (New York: Mentor, 1960), pp. 44–49; Daniel T. Kevles, *In the Name of Eugenics* (Berkeley: University of California Press, 1985), pp. 40–45 and passim.

7. Starting with a given pair of forebears, it is more probable, according to Mendelian heredity, that offspring will have some genetic combinations rather than others, i.e., more probable that the individual with two mulatto parents will get some white racial genes than no white racial genes. But this concept of probability is a statistical aspect of heredity that yields no certainty in individual cases; and when people categorize other people racially, they do so as if the categorization were certain in individual cases. See Dunn and Dobzhansky, *Heredity, Race and Society*, pp. 45, 73, and 136–40, for discussions of genetic probabilities.

8. See Kevles, *Name of Eugenics*, pp. 266–67, 294–95, 297, for discussions of mapping.

9. In fact, Caroline Bond Day, in her detailed 1931 study of twenty-five hundred individuals of mixed black and white race, found that individuals who were more than one-half black appeared clearly to be so. But individuals who were mulattoes or "one-half" black could be divided into three groups: Some appeared more black than they were ancestrally; some had a "balanced" array of black and white traits; some seemed to have a predominance of white traits. Day thought that there was a "natural tendency" for white physical traits to dominate. Thus, she said, quadroons never combined in one person all three Negroid traits of "frizzly hair, swarthy skin and heavy facial features." All quadroons she observed were

"easily" able to pass for white and all octoroons she observed had no visible trace of their black ancestry. Day's findings are cited by Williamson, *New People*, pp. 125–26.

10. See Carl N. Degler, *Neither Black nor White* (New York: Macmillan, 1971), pp. 103–4.

11. See Oliver C. Cox, *Caste, Class and Race* (New York: Doubleday, 1959), pp. 360–62.

12. Ibid., pp. 384–86.

13. Cf. James Kinney, *Amalgamation!* (Westport, Conn.: Greenwood, 1985), pp. 10–11.

14. For example, the Census Bureau in 1918 estimated that roughly three-quarters of the Negro population were mixed black and white race. See Williamson, *New People*, p. 125.

Chapter 8

1. See Robert J. Sickels, *Race, Marriage and the Law* (Albuquerque: University of New Mexico Press, 1972), pp. 1–10.

2. Ibid., p. 64.

3. Ibid. Cited by Sickels from the *New York Times*, March 16, 1964, sec. 4, p. 12.

4. This is a truism in the literature on the subject of miscegenation. See, e.g., James Kinney, *Amalgamation!* (Westport, Conn.: Greenwood, 1985), pp. 7–8.

5. Cited in Kinney, *Amalgamation!* pp. 7–8; from Gunnar Myrdal, *An American Dilemma* (New York: Harper, 1944), p. 56. Myrdal's work is now out of print, and Myrdal out of favor. Myrdal was overly optimistic about the prognosis for race relations in the United States. He predicted that American egalitarian ideals and rationality would ultimately overcome racism. See R. Fred Wacker, *Ethnicity, Pluralism and Race* (Westport, Conn.: Greenwood, 1983), pp. 83–85. Regarding Myrdal's 1944 observation of the asymmetry in attitudes against miscegenation, it is interesting to note that the 1991 movie *Jungle Fever*, directed by Spike Lee, was deemed "highly controversial" because its subject is a love affair between a black man and a white woman. This love affair ends, in large part due to racial prejudice by both blacks and whites.

6. Kinney, *Amalgamation!* pp. 8–9, 114; see also the foreword to Kinney's work by John W. Blassingame, Sr., and Henry Louis Gates, Jr., p. xii.

7. Joel Williamson, *New People* (New York: Free Press, 1980), p. 7; Kinney, *Amalgamation!* pp. 4–5.

8. Cited by Kinney, *Amalgamation!* p. 5.

9. Kinney, *Amalgamation!* p. 5.

10. Williamson, *New People*, p. 8.

11. Kinney, *Amalgamation!* p. 5.

12. Williamson, *New People*, p. 10.

13. Ibid.

14. Ibid., pp. 10–11.

15. Kinney, *Amalgamation!* p. 4; Williamson, *New People*, p. 12; *World Almanac* (New York: Pharos Books, 1990), p. 551.

16. Ibid.

17. Williamson, *New People*, pp. 9–10.

18. Ibid.

19. Ibid., pp. 13–14.

20. Ibid., pp. 24–25.

21. Ibid., p. 26.

22. Ibid., pp. 14–15, 27–29; John G. Mencke, *Mulattoes and Race Mixture* (Ann Arbor: University of Michigan Institute of Research Press, 1979), pp. 10–13.

23. Kinney, *Amalgamation!* p. 11.

24. Williamson, *New People*, p. 29.

25. Mencke, *Mulattoes and Race Mixture*, pp. 9–10; Williamson, *New People*, p. 14.

26. Kinney, *Amalgamation!* pp. 23–24.

27. Mencke, *Mulattoes and Race Mixture*, p. 20.

28. Williamson, *New People*, pp. 63, 71–75.

29. Cited by Mencke, *Mulattoes and Race Mixture*, p. 18; from Henry Hughes, *Treatise on Sociology, Theoretical and Practical* (New York: Lippincott, Crambo & Co., 1854), p. 31.

30. Mencke, *Mulattoes and Race Mixture*, p. 14.

31. Kinney, *Amalgamation!* p. 11.

32. Mencke, *Mulattoes and Race Mixture*, p. 27; Williamson, *New People*, pp. 63–65.

33. Williamson, *New People*, p. 114.

34. Ibid., pp. 98–99.

35. Mencke, *Mulattoes and Race Mixture*, p. 28.

36. See Williamson's discussion of the obsession with racial purity and his discussion of the speculations about passing in *New People*, pp. 100–104.

37. Mencke, *Mulattoes and Race Mixture*, p. 37; from Booker T. Washington, *The Future of the American Negro* (Boston: Small, Maynard and Co., 1900), p. 158.

38. By 1967 the punishment for interracial marriage varied greatly: Fines were between fifty dollars (in Colorado) and five thousand dollars (Kentucky); imprisonment ranged from one month (Arkansas) to ten years (Mississippi, Indiana, Florida, and South Dakota). In some states both partners were punished, and in others only the white partner. See Beth Day, *Sexual Life between Blacks and Whites* (New York: World Publishing, 1972), p. 99; Williamson, *New People*, p. 94.

Chapter 9

1. Frazier did not use the word "maroon"; nor did he seem to be aware of the concept. See "Racial Islands," in E. Franklin Frazier, *The Negro Family in the United States* (Chicago: University of Chicago Press, 1973), pp. 164–89.

2. For these definitions, see, e.g., *Webster's New Collegiate Dictionary*, 2d ed. (1960), s.v. "maroon"; and *The Concise Oxford English Dictionary*, 5th ed. (1964), s.v. "maroon."

3. Frazier, *Negro Family*, p. 165. Frazier's account of the "racial islands," discussed in this chapter, can be found in *Negro Family*, pp. 165–84.

4. Ibid., p. 188.

5. Ibid., p. 179.

6. Ibid., pp. 176–77.

7. Ibid., p. 368.

8. Ibid., p. 189.

Chapter 10

1. Joel Williamson, *New People* (New York: Free Press, 1980), pp. 112, 113. The 1910 census data was not officially reported until 1918 and it included a survey by the Census Bureau taken over decades. By 1920 the mulatto count was down to 15.9 percent (as opposed to the 1910 figure of 20.9 percent of the Negro population).

2. Ibid., p. 111.

3. See W.E.B. Du Bois, "The Talented Tenth," in idem, *Essays and Articles*, reprinted in *Du Bois Writings*, comp. Nathan Huggins (New York: Literary Classics of the U.S., 1986), pp. 842–61.

4. Williamson, *New People*, p. 129.

5. See Ibid., p. 161; Willard B. Gatewood, *Aristocrats of Color* (Bloomington and Indianapolis: Indiana University Press, 1990), pp. 3–29.

6. Williamson, *New People*, p. 109; Gatewood, *Aristocrats of Color*, pp. 319–22, 347–48.

7. See, e.g., Zora Neale Hurston, *Dirt Tracks on a Road* (New York: Lippincott, 1942), pp. 223–46. Hurston concludes this chapter on *diversity* in her autobiography with these words: "Our lives are so diversified, internal attitudes so varied, appearance and capabilities so different, that there is no possible classification so catholic that it will cover us all, except My People! My People!"

Also, as Cary D. Wintz notes, not all of the participants in the Harlem Renaissance acknowledged it as such. See Cary D. Wintz, *Black Culture and the Harlem Renaissance* (Houston: Rice University Press, 1988), p. 2.

8. Williamson, *New People*, p. 2. Williamson refers to Horace Mann Bond's 1930 statement that there had been no "ripple of amusement" at a recent meeting where a "blue-eyed Anglo Saxon" speaker asserted "the necessity that all of us black men in America and the world stand together."

9. From the late nineteenth century on, there was an increase in miscegenation among blacks that consisted of the visible mulattoes marrying darker-skinned blacks. This type of miscegentation in no small part led to a change in the physical racial characteristics of the majority of people who were called "Negroes." See Williamson, *New People*, pp. 123–28.

10. See Wintz, *Black Culture*, p. 226. Although the Harlem Renaissance had white promoters, publishers, and patrons and most of the book-buying public was white, the work of the Harlem Renaissance did not become part of mainstream artistic and intellectual American culture, much less a subject of interest for the majority of the white American population. (See also pp. 87–217.)

11. Langston Hughes voiced the motive of safety through his character Simple in *Simple Speaks His Mind*: "What is it you love about Harlem?" the writer asked his friend Jesse B. Simple over drinks at the bar. "It's so full of Negroes," said Simple. "I feel like I got protection." "From what?" "From white folks." (Cited by Williamson, *New People*, p. 141.)

12. Wintz, *Black Culture*, pp. 13–14. The following overview of the climate for blacks in Harlem and elsewhere in the United States from the 1890s to 1930 can be found in Wintz, *Black Culture*, pp. 7–27.

13. Langston Hughes, *Simple Speaks His Mind*, reprinted in *Langston Hughes Reader* (New York: George Braziller, 1958), p. 201. Hughes wrote this in 1953, and there is no reason to believe it did not apply to 1923.

14. Williamson, *New People*, pp. 134–35.

15. E.g., see Robert J. Sickels, *Race, Marriage and the Law* (Albuquerque: University of New Mexico Press, 1972), p. 72.

16. Williamson, *New People*, pp. 112–13.

17. Ibid., pp. 123, 125, 127.

18. Ibid., pp. 134, 163, 184.

19. Wintz, *Black Culture*, pp. 48–87.

20. Ibid., pp. 30–31, 47.

21. Williamson, *New People*, pp. 145–51.

22. Booker T. Washington, *Up from Slavery*, reprinted in John Hope Franklin, ed., *Three Negro Classics* (New York: Avon Books, 1965), pp. 30, 95.

23. Williamson, *New People*, p. 86.

24. Ibid., pp. 151–52.

25. Ibid., p. 192.

26. See Du Bois, *Du Bois Writings*, p. 570.

27. Williamson, *New People*, p. 102; Gatewood, *Aristocrats of Color*, p. 309 and passim.

28. See W.E.B. Du Bois, review of Van Vechten's *Nigger Heaven*, idem, *Du Bois Writings*, pp. 1216–18. See also Wintz, *Black Culture*, pp. 100–102, 130, 140–47.

29. Wintz, *Black Culture*, pp. 140–47.

30. Du Bois first made this color line statement in a 1900 speech; see *Du Bois Writings*, p. 1288. See also p. 359 for his introductory reference to the veil in *The Souls of Black Folk*.

31. About dual consciousness, see, e.g., Charles Vert Willie, *The Ivory and Ebony Towers* (Lexington, Mass.: Lexington Books, 1981), pp. 7–15; Du Bois, *Souls of Black Folk*, in idem, *Du Bois Writings*, pp. 364–65.

32. For example, when he traveled through the South in 1934, he always packed a lunch and carried a car repair kit so he would not have to stop at white-owned establishments. See Du Bois, *Du Bois Writings*, p. 1298.

It is commonly acknowledged that Du Bois securely saw himself as part of the black race. See, e.g., Williamson, *New People*, p. 102;

W.E.B. Du Bois, *Dusk of Dawn*, in idem, *Du Bois Writings*, pp. 652–715.

33. These lines by Countee Cullen suggest that he felt that being black was opposed to being a poet:

Yet do I marvel at this curious thing:

To make a poet black, and bid him sing.

(Cited by Williamson, *New People*, p. 167.) As Williamson describes Cullen, he could be white as well as black, and white in the white world.

Jean Toomer is sometimes discussed as a writer who wrote about blackness in a white way even though he was black, or who wrote in a way that made his color irrelevant, which some black critics would consider to be the same thing. See, e.g., Waldo Frank's foreword in Jean Toomer, *Cane* (New York: Liveright, 1975), pp. vii–xi.

34. W.E.B. Du Bois, *Dusk of Dawn*, in idem, *Du Bois Writings*, p. 561; see also p. 1281. The following biographical material on Du Bois comes from *Du Bois Writings*, pp. 560–70.

35. Du Bois, *Du Bois Writings*, p. 170.

36. Wintz, *Black Culture*, p. 88.

37. Hurston, *Dirt Tracks*, pp. 11–19.

38. Williamson, *New People*, 153–54; Gatewood, *Aristocrats of Color*, pp. 309–11.

39. Wintz, *Black Culture*, pp. 213–16.

40. Ibid., pp. 116–18.

41. Williamson, *New People*, pp. 154–56.

42. Hurston, *Dirt Tracks*, p. 263.

43. Ibid., pp. 242–43.

44. Ibid., p. 244.

45. See Langston Hughes, *The Big Sea*, in idem, *Langston Hughes Reader*, pp. 381–88, for Hughes's assessment of the Harlem Renaissance that follows.

46. Ibid., pp. 322–23.

47. Ibid., pp. 323, 342; Williamson, *New People*, p. 146.

48. Hughes, *Big Sea*, in idem, *Langston Hughes Reader*, p. 322.

49. Williamson, *New People*, pp. 147–50.

50. Toomer, *Cane*, pp. 18–19.

51. Williamson, *New People*, p. 150.

52. Hughes, *Big Sea*, in idem, *Langston Hughes Reader*, pp. 379–81.

53. Wintz, *Black Culture*, p. 117.

54. Hughes, *Big Sea*, in idem, *Langston Hughes Reader*, p. 380.

55. See Richard Rorty, *Contingency, Irony and Solidarity* (Cambridge: Cambridge University Press, 1988), pp. 73–83.

56. See *Secret Talks with Mr. G.* (IDHHB, 1978), pp. 124–36.

Chapter 11

1. Ambrose Bierce, *The Devil's Dictionary* (New York: Dover, 1958), p. 90.

2. For example these entries appear: "AFRICAN, *n.* A nigger that votes our way" (ibid., p. 10); "NEGRO, *n.* The *piece de resistance* in the American political problem. Representing him by the letter *n* the Republicans begin to build their equation thus: 'Let *n* = the white man.' This, however, appears to give an unsatisfactory solution" (p. 90).

3. Joel Williamson, *New People* (New York: Free Press, 1980), pp. 116–18.

4. See Chapter 10, n. 3, above.

5. Williamson, *New People*, pp. 149–50.

6. See John C. Mencke, *Mulattoes and Race Mixture* (Ann Arbor: University of Michigan Institute of Research Press, 1979), pp. 22–24.

7. See Booker T. Washington, *Up from Slavery*, reprinted in John Hope Franklin, ed., *Three Negro Classics* (New York: Avon, 1965), pp. 145–50.

8. Mencke, *Mulattoes and Race Mixture*, pp. 124–32.

9. Williamson, *New People*, pp. 18–19.

10. Ibid., p. 93.

11. Ibid., pp. 33, 43; Ann Rice *The Feast of All Saints* (New York: Random House, 1986).

12. Mencke, *Mulattoes and Race Mixture*, pp. 127–29.

13. Cited by Mencke, *Mulattoes and Race Mixture*, p. 105.

14. Ibid., p. 106.

15. Ibid., p. 102.

16. Ibid., pp. 111–12.

17. Ibid., pp. 78–83.

18. Ibid., p. 109.

19. Ibid., pp. 102–3.

20. Williamson, *New People*, pp. 92–93.

21. Cited by Mencke, *Mulattoes and Race Mixture*, p. 103.

22. Ibid., pp. 57–58.

23. Cited by Robert J. Sickels, *Race, Marriage and the Law* (Albuquerque: University of New Mexico Press, 1972), pp. 40–41.

24. Ibid., pp. 57–58.

25. Williamson, *New People*, pp. 95–96.

26. Mencke, *Mulattoes and Race Mixture*, pp. 39–40.

27. Ibid., pp. 86–87.

28. Ibid., pp. 39–46.

29. Ibid., pp. 46–50; Pitzer's statement cited p. 117.

30. Cited by Mencke, *Mulattoes and Race Mixture*, p. 119.

31. Mencke, *Mulattoes and Race Mixture*, p. 73.

32. L. C. Dunn and Theodosius Dobzhansky, *Heredity, Race and Society* (New York: Mentor, 1960), pp. 118–31.

33. Mencke, *Mulattoes and Race Mixture*, pp. 66, 71, 72; see also R. Fred Wacker, *Ethnicity, Pluralism and Race* (Westport, Conn.: Greenwood, 1983), pp. 15, 17, 22, 79.

34. Sickels, *Race, Marriage, Law*, pp. 53–54.

35. Ibid., p. 54.

36. Ibid., pp. 45–46, 49.

37. Mencke, *Mulattoes and Race Mixture*, pp. 115–16; Williamson, *New People*, pp. 71–73.

38. Mencke, *Mulattoes and Race Mixture*, pp. 37–43; Sickels, *Race, Marriage, Law*, p. 56.

39. Williamson, *New People*, pp. 94–95.

40. Cited by Sickels, *Race, Marriage, Law*, pp. 54–55.

41. Williamson, *New People*, pp. 92–94.

42. Mencke, *Mulattoes and Race Mixture*, pp. 49, 51, 59, 60, 64.

43. Ibid., pp. 129–31.

44. Ibid., pp. 124–28.

45. Williamson, *New People*, pp. 92–94.

46. E. Franklin Frazier, *The Negro Family in the United States* (Chicago: University of Chicago Press, 1973), p. 235.

47. Williamson, *New People*, p. 14; Sickels, *Race, Marriage, Law*, pp. 34–35, 37, 42.

48. Cited by Mencke, *Mulattoes and Race Mixture*, p. 106.

49. Williamson, *New People*, pp. 188–90; Sickels, *Race, Marriage, Law*, p. 132.

50. Beth Day, *Sexual Life between Blacks and Whites* (New York: World Publishing, 1972), pp. 304, 339–53.

51. See *I-Pride Newsletter* 15, no. 1 (Jan. 1993): 20–21 (published by I-Pride in San Francisco).

Chapter 12

1. Friedrich Nietzsche, *On the Genealogy of Morals* (New York: Vintage Books, 1969), third essay, sec. 5, p. 102.

2. See John C. Mencke, *Mulattoes and Race Mixture* (Ann Arbor: University of Michigan Institute of Research Press, 1979), pp. 141–233.

3. See James Kinney, *Amalgamation!* (Westport, Conn.: Greenwood, 1985), pp. 3–35, 225–35.

4. See Eric J. Sundquist, *Faulkner: The House Divided* (Baltimore: Johns Hopkins University Press, 1983), pp. 63–96.

5. Cited by Mencke, *Mulattoes and Race Mixture*, p. 148.

6. Ibid., p. 218.

7. Kinney, *Amalgamation!* pp. 62–93.

8. Mencke, *Mulattoes and Race Mixture*, pp. 141–63.

9. Ibid., pp. 193–205; Kinney, *Amalgamation!* pp. 93–97, 108–9.

10. Mencke, p. 192.

11. Ibid., p. 213.

12. Ibid., pp. 143–45.

13. Ibid., pp. 208.

14. Ibid., p. 204.

15. Cited by Mencke, *Mulattoes and Race Mixture*, pp. 171–72.

16. See Kinney, *Amalgamation!*, p. 218.

17. See Kinney, *Amalgamation!* pp. 220–22.

18. Ibid.

19. See Jonathan Bennett, "The Conscience of Huckleberry Finn," in Christina Sommers and Fred Sommers, eds., *Vice and Virtue in Everyday Life* (New York: Harcourt Brace Jovanovich, 1989), pp. 25–40.

20. James Weldon Johnson, *Autobiography of an Ex-Colored Man*, reprinted in John Hope Franklin, ed., *Three Negro Classics* (New York: Avon, 1965), pp. 510–11.

21. Jean Toomer, *Cane* (New York: Liveright, 1975), pp. 144–46.

22. Ibid., p. 141.

23. See, e.g., Homi K. Bhabha, "Interrogating Identity: The Postcolonial Prerogative," in David Theo Goldberg, ed., *Anatomy of Racism* (Minneapolis: University of Minnesota Press, 1990), pp. 183–209.

24. Franz Fanon, "The Fact of Blackness," in Goldberg, ed., *Anatomy of Racism*, p. 110.

25. Cf. Langston Hughes, *The Big Sea* in idem, *Langston Hughes Reader* (New York: George Braziller, 1958), pp. 348–49.

26. Toomer, *Cane*, p. 149.

27. Sherwood Anderson reported conversations in which Faulkner repeated obvious myths about race; see Joel Williamson, *New People* (New York: Free Press, 1980), pp. 96–97.

28. William Faulkner, *Light in August* (New York: Modern Library, 1968), pp. 439–40.

29. Nietzsche, *Genealogy of Morals*, third essay, sec. 4, p. 101.

30. Toni Morrison, *The Bluest Eye* (New York: Washington Square, 1970), pp. 9, 107–27.

31. Ibid., pp. 86–87.

32. Ibid., pp. 126–29.

33. Ibid., pp. 72–75.

34. Ibid., pp. 132–33.

Chapter 13

1. For specific references to the racism against Africans, for example, in the writing of David Hume, Immanuel Kant, G.W.F. Hegel, and Friedrich Engels, see Tsenay Serequeberhan, "African Philosophy: The Point in Question," in idem, ed., *African Philosophy* (New York: Paragon, 1991), pp. 4–8.

2. See Zora Neal Hurston, *Dirt Tracks on a Road* (New York: Lippincott, 1942), pp. 242–44.

Chapter 14

1. By "parody" he meant "to sing along with." He thought that I might have been "appropriating" Heidegger for no clear or worthy purpose.

2. Martin Heidegger, "The Spiegel Interview," in Gunther Neske and Emil Kettering, eds., *Martin Heidegger and National Socialism* (New York: Paragon, 1990), p. 63.

3. Martin Heidegger, "The Rectoral Address" and "The Self Assertion of the German University," in Neske and Kettering, eds., *Heidegger and National Socialism*, pp. 6–8 and 62–63; Hans Jonas, "Heidegger's Resoluteness and Resolve," in Neske and Kettering, eds., *Heidegger and National Socialism*, pp. 200–202. On the issue of translating *Being and Time* into Spanish, see Hugo Ott, "Paths and Wrong Paths," in Neske and Kettering, eds., *Heidegger and National Socialism*, p. 135.

4. See Martin Heidegger, "The Question Concerning Technology," in idem, *The Question Concerning Technology and Other Essays* (New York: Harper & Row, 1977), pp. 3–21, 32–35.

5. See, e.g., Heidegger, "The Spiegel Interview," in Neske and Kettering, eds., *Heidegger and National Socialism*, pp. 55–66.

6. See, e.g., John Searle, "The Battle over the University," *New York Review of Books* 37, no. 19 (Dec. 1990): 34–43.

7. Martin Bernal, *Black Athena* (New Brunswick, N.J.: Rutgers University Press, 1987), pp. 439–45.

8. On revenge, see Alexander Theroux, "Revenge," in Christina Sommers and Fred Sommers, eds., *Vice and Virtue in Everyday Life* (New York: Harcourt Brace Jovanovich, 1989), pp. 359–70.

9. Friedrich Nietzsche, *Beyond Good and Evil*, reprinted in *Basic Writings of Nietzsche* (New York: Modern Library, 1968), no. 260, pp. 395–96.

10. Ibid., no. 262, pp. 400–401.

11. Jean-Paul Sartre, *Anti-Semite and Jew* (New York: Schocken, 1965), pp. 7–9; R. M. Hare, *Freedom and Reason* (Oxford: Clarendon, 1987), pp. 157–86.

12. Sartre, *Anti-Semite and Jew*, p. 23.

13. Ibid., pp. 19–20.

14. Ibid., p. 18.

15. Ibid., pp. 19–20.

16. Ibid., p. 26.

17. Ibid., pp. 35–40.

18. Ibid., pp. 40–45.

19. Ibid., pp. 50–54.

20. Ibid., pp. 94–104.

21. Ibid., p. 146.

22. Ibid., p. 141.

23. Franz Fanon, "The Fact of Blackness," in David Theo Goldberg, ed., *Anatomy of Racism* (Minneapolis: University of Minnesota Press, 1990), pp. 121, 123–24.

24. Liliane Siegel, *In the Shadow of Sartre* (London: Collins, 1990), pp. 69–83.

25. Sartre, *Anti-Semite and Jew*, p. 119.

Chapter 15

1. Contemporary Black Identity Theory holds that all designated black individuals experience predictable stages in developing black identities as part of their value-positive emancipation. See, e.g., William S. Hall, Roy Freedle, and William E. Cross, Jr., *Stages in the Development*

of a Black Identity (Iowa City: Research and Development Division, American College Teaching Program, 1972). This theory omits the possibilities that individuals of mixed race may never acquire black identities and that it may not be necessary or even desirable for them to do so in order to achieve full, value-positive emancipation.

2. See R. Fred Wacker, *Ethnicity, Pluralism and Race* (Westport, Conn.: Greenwood, 1983), pp. 13–40.

3. William Rubin, ed., *Pablo Picasso* (New York: Museum of Modern Art, 1980), p. 353.

4. See, e.g., Martha Weinman Lear, "The Second Feminist Wave," in June Sochen, ed., *The New Feminism in Twentieth-Century America* (Lexington, Mass.: D. C. Heath, 1971), pp. 161–72.

5. See Michael Leiris, "Race and Culture," in Leo Kuper, ed., *Race, Science and Society* (New York: Columbia University Press, 1965), pp. 135–72.

6. Ibid., p. 159. See also the United Nations statements on the "Race Question" between 1950 and 1967, which restate Leiris's main theme that culture is not physically inherited, in Kuper, ed., *Race, Science and Society*, Appendix.

7. For example, the bull and several of the other figures in *Guernica* were developed in earlier paintings and drawings by Picasso. See Charles Harrison, "Picasso's Guernica," in *Images of The Spanish Civil War* (Walton Hall, England: Open University Press, 1981), pp. 101–25.

8. Richard Rorty, *Contingency, Irony and Solidarity* (Cambridge: Cambridge University Press, 1988), p. xv.

9. Ibid., pp. 23–44, 77.

10. According to H. P. Grice, normal communication presupposes cooperation. On the assumption of cooperation, if certain obvious rules of discourse are broken, the listener has reason to infer a logical implication behind what the speaker has literally said. For example, if we are cooperating and I ask you how X's performance was last night and you tell me that X knew all her lines, I can infer, according to the Rule of Relevance, that X's performance was not very good, because you have flouted the Rule of Relevance. See H. P. Grice, "Logic and Conversation," in Donald Davidson and Gilbert Harman, eds., *The Logic of Grammar* (Encino, Calif.: Dickinson, 1975), pp. 64–153. Insults, especially racial insults and implied racial insults, do not merely flout the normal rules but signal that cooperation in communication is not present. This may be why insults lead so easily to acts of violence, i.e., they signal that verbal communication is no longer possible.

11. See John L. Hodge, "Equality: Beyond Dualism and Oppression," in David Theo Goldberg, ed., *Anatomy of Racism* (Minneapolis: University of Minnesota Press, 1990), pp. 89–108.

12. See Carl N. Degler, *Neither Black nor White* (Madison: University of Wisconsin Press, 1986), p. xviii.

13. See *Webster's New Collegiate Dictionary*, 2d ed. (1960), s.v. "Caucasian," "Negro."

14. See Degler, *Neither Black nor White*, p. 277.

15. William Cecil Dampier, *A History of Science* (Cambridge: Cambridge University Press, 1943), p. 176.

16. See Degler, *Neither Black nor White*, pp. 105–7.

17. Not only was there, in Brazil, a lack of interest in breeding slaves, as compared to the United States, but manumission was easier and more frequent in Brazil, especially in the case of slaves of mixed race. See ibid., pp. 19–20, 39–47, 61–67.

18. Henry Louis Gates, Jr., "Critical Remarks," in Goldberg, ed., *Anatomy of Racism*, p. 332.

19. Degler, *Neither Black nor White*, pp. 102–3; John C. Mencke, *Mulattoes and Race Mixture* (Ann Arbor: University of Michigan Institute of Research Press, 1979), pp. ix, 2–3; Joel Williamson, *New People* (New York: Free Press, 1980), pp. 23–24. It should be noted that the old racial words for mixed black and white race, e.g., "quadroon," "octaroon," etc., are no more naturalistically descriptive than the words for people who are racially pure.

20. The nineteenth-century fiction sympathetic to mulattoes was replete with such descriptions. Many writers claim that among contemporary American blacks, close attention is paid to gradations in skin color. See, e.g., Beth Day, *Sexual Life between Blacks and Whites* (New York: World, 1972), pp. 185–87. Also, there is a tradition in black letters of aesthetic racial pride, based on the variation in appearance among people who are designated as black in the United States. See W.E.B. Du Bois, *The Dusk of Dawn*, in idem, *Du Bois Writings*, comp. Nathan Huggins (New York: Literary Classics of the U.S., 1986), pp. 657–58.

Select Bibliography

Books (Monographs and Anthologies)

Ashworth, Georgina, ed. *World Minorities*. 3 vol. Sunberry, England: Quartermaine, 1977, 1978, 1980.

Baxter, Angus. *In Search of Your Roots*. Toronto: Macmillan, 1972.

Bell, Derrick. *And We Are Not Saved*. New York: Basic Books, 1987.

Bernal, Martin. *Black Athena*. New Brunswick, N.J.: Rutgers University Press, 1987.

Bordo, Susan. *The Flight to Objectivity*. Albany: State University of New York Press, 1987.

Breeden, James O., ed. *Advice to Masters: The Ideal in Slave Management in the Old South*. Westport, Conn.: Greenwood, 1980.

Cashmore, E. Ellis, and Barry Troyman. *Introduction to Race Relations*. London: Routledge & Kegan Paul, 1983.

Cox, Oliver C. *Caste, Class and Race*, New York: Doubleday, 1959.

Davis, Lenwood G., comp. *The Black Family in the United States*. New York: Greenwood, 1986.

Day, Beth. *Sexual Life between Blacks and Whites*. New York: World, 1972.

Degler, Carl N. *Neither Black nor White*. Madison: University of Wisconsin Press, 1986.

Du Bois, W.E.B. *Du Bois Writings*. Compiled by Nathan Huggins. New York: Literary Classics of the U.S., 1986.

———, ed. *Negro American Family*. New York: Negro University Press, 1969.

Entries under "Essays and Articles" and "Fiction" sections with incomplete sources can be found under "Books" in the anthologies.

Dunn, L. C., and Theodosius Dobzhansky. *Heredity, Race and Society.* New York: Mentor, 1960.

Finley, M. I. *Ancient Slavery and Modern Ideology.* New York: Pelican, 1983.

Franklin, John Hope, ed. *Three Negro Classics.* New York: Avon, 1965.

Frazier, E. Franklin. *The Negro Family in the United States.* Chicago: University of Chicago Press, 1973.

Gatewood, Willard B. *Aristocrats of Color.* Bloomington and Indianapolis: Indiana University Press, 1990.

Goldberg, David Theo, ed. *Anatomy of Racism.* Minneapolis: University of Minnesota Press, 1990.

Gwaltney, John Langston. *Drylongso.* New York: Random House, 1980.

Hall, William S., Roy Freedle, and William E. Cross, Jr. *Stages in the Development of a Black Identity.* Iowa City: Research and Development Division, American College Teaching Program, 1972.

Hare, Nathan, and Julia Hare. *The Endangered Black Family.* San Francisco: Black Think Tank, 1984.

Heidegger, Martin. *Being and Time.* Translated by John MacQuarrie and Edward Robinson. New York: Harper & Row, 1962.

———. *The Question Concerning Technology.* Translated by William Lovitt. New York: Harper Torchbooks, 1977.

Hughes, Langston. *Langston Hughes Reader.* New York: George Braziller, 1958.

Hurston, Zora Neale. *Dirt Tracks on a Road.* New York: Lippincott, 1942.

Kevles, Daniel T. *In the Name of Eugenics.* Berkeley: University of California Press, 1985.

Kinney, James. *Amalgamation!* Westport, Conn.: Greenwood, 1985.

Kuper, Leo, ed., *Race, Science and Society.* New York: Columbia University Press, 1965.

Locke, John. *Second Treatise on Government.* Edited by William S. Carpenter. London: J. M. Dent & Sons, 1989.

Mencke, John C. *Mulattoes and Race Mixture.* Ann Arbor: University of Michigan Institute of Research Press, 1979.

Nagel, Thomas. *The View from Nowhere.* New York: Oxford University Press, 1986.

Neske, Gunther, and Emil Kettering, eds. *Martin Heidegger and National Socialism.* New York: Paragon, 1990.

Nicholson, Linda. *Gender and History.* New York: Columbia University Press, 1986.

Nietzsche, Friedrich. *On the Genealogy of Morals*. New York: Vintage Books, 1969.

Nobles, Wade W., and Lawford L. Goddard. *Understanding the Black Family*. Oakland, Calif.: The Institute for the Advanced Study of Black Family Life and Culture, 1984.

Pleasant, William, ed. *Independent Black Leadership in America*. New York: Castillo International Publications, 1990.

Reich, Wilhelm. *Character Analysis: The Function of the Orgasm*. New York: Farrar, Straus & Giroux, 1958.

———. *The Mass Psychology of Fascism*. New York: Farrar, Straus & Giroux, 1970.

Rex, John. *Race and Ethnicity*. Storey Stratford, England: Open University Press, 1986.

Ridgeway, James. *Blood in the Face*. New York: Thundermouth, 1990.

Rorty, Richard. *Contingency, Irony and Solidarity*. Cambridge: Cambridge University Press, 1988.

Sartre, Jean-Paul. *Anti-Semite and Jew*. New York: Schocken, 1965.

Serequeberhan, Tsenay, ed. *African Philosophy*. New York: Paragon, 1991.

Sickels, Robert J. *Race, Marriage and the Law*. Albuquerque: University of New Mexico Press, 1972.

Siegel, Liliane. *In the Shadow of Sartre*. London: Collins, 1990.

Sommers, Christina, and Fred Sommers, eds. *Vice and Virtue in Everyday Life*. New York: Harcourt Brace Jovanovich, 1989.

Squibb, G. D. *Founders' Kin*. Oxford: Oxford University Press, 1972.

Stone, Elizabeth. *Black Sheep and Kissing Cousins*. New York: Penguin, 1989.

Sundquist, Eric J. *Faulkner: The House Divided*. Baltimore: Johns Hopkins University Press, 1983.

Wacker, R. Fred. *Ethnicity, Pluralism and Race*. Westport, Conn.: Greenwood, 1983.

Wiedemann, Thomas. *Greek and Roman Slavery*. Baltimore: Johns Hopkins University Press, 1981.

Williams, Patricia J. *The Alchemy of Race and Rights*. Cambridge: Harvard University Press, 1991.

Williamson, Joel. *New People*. New York: Free Press, 1980.

Willie, Charles Vert. *The Ivory and Ebony Towers*. Lexington, Mass.: Lexington Books, 1981.

Wintz, Cary D. *Black Culture and the Harlem Renaissance*. Houston: Rice University Press, 1988.

Essays and Articles

Appiah, Anthony. "'But Would That Still Be Me?': Notes on Gender, 'Race', Ethnicity as Sources of Identity," *Journal of Philosophy* 77, no. 10 (Oct. 1990): 493–500.

———. "Racisms." In Goldberg, ed., *Anatomy of Racism*.

Arendt, Hannah. "For Martin Heidegger's Eightieth Birthday." In Neske and Kettering, eds., *Heidegger and Naitonal Socialism*.

Baier, Annette. "A Naturalistic View of Persons." *APA Proceedings and Addresses* 65, no. 3 (Nov. 1991): 5–17.

Bennett, Jonathan. "The Conscience of Huckleberry Finn." In Sommers and Sommers, eds., *Vice and Virtue*.

Bhabha, Homi K. "Interrogating Identity: The Postcolonial Prerogative." In Goldberg, ed., *Anatomy of Racism*.

Bracy, John H. "The Black Middle Class: Help or Hindrance." In *The Black Middle Class: Proceedings of a Conference at Skidmore College*. Edited by Mary C. Lynn and Benjamin D. Berry. Saratoga Springs, N.Y.: Skidmore College, 1980.

Christian, Barbara. "What Celie Knows That You Should Know." In Goldberg, ed., *Anatomy of Racism*.

Dubinin, N. P. "Race and Contemporary Genetics." In Kuper, ed., *Race, Science and Society*.

Du Bois, W.E.B. *The Dusk of Dawn; Essays and Articles; The Souls of Black Folk*. In Du Bois, *Du Bois Writings*.

Dunn, L. C. "Race and Biology." In Kuper, ed., *Race, Science and Society*.

Fanon, Franz. "The Fact of Blackness." In Goldberg, ed., *Anatomy of Racism*.

Farrakhan, Louis. "Interview in *National Alliance* Newspaper." In Pleasant, ed., *Independent Black Leadership*.

Fulani, Lenora. "Fulani." In Pleasant, ed., *Independent Black Leadership*.

Gates, Henry Louis, Jr. "Critical Remarks." In Goldberg, ed., *Anatomy of Racism*.

Gens, Walter. "Words in Memory of Martin Heidegger from the Academy of the Arts in Berlin." In Neske and Kettering, eds., *Heidegger and National Socialism*.

Gluckman, Max. "New Dimensions of Change, Conflict and Settlement." In Kuper, ed., *Race, Science and Society*.

Goldberg, David Theo. "The Social Formation of Fascist Discourse." In Goldberg, ed., *Anatomy of Racism*.

Grice, H. P. "Logic and Conversation." In *The Logic of Grammar*. Edited by Donald Davidson and Gilbert Harman. Encino, Calif.: Dickinson, 1975.

Heidegger, Martin. "The Rectoral Address"; "The Self Assertion of the German University"; "The Spiegel Interview"; "The Television Interview." In Neske and Kettering, eds., *Heidegger and National Socialism*.

Hodge, John L. "Equality: Beyond Dualism and Oppression." In Goldberg, ed., *Anatomy of Racism*.

Hughes, Langston. *The Big Sea; Simple Speaks His Mind*. In Hughes, *Langston Hughes Reader*.

Jonas, Hans. "Heidegger's Resoluteness and Resolve." In Neske and Kettering, eds., *Heidegger and National Socialism*.

Klineberg, Otto. "Race and Psychology." In Kuper, ed., *Race, Science and Society*.

Lear, Martha Weinman. "The Second Feminist Wave." In *The New Feminism in Twentieth-Century America*. Edited by June Sochen. Lexington, Mass.: D.C. Heath, 1971.

Leiris, Michael. "Race and Culture." In Kuper, ed., *Race, Science and Society*.

Lloyd, Genevieve. "The Man of Reason." In *Women, Knowledge and Reality*. Edited by Ann Garry and Marilyn Pearsall. Boston: Unwin Hyman, 1989.

Oruka, Henry Odera. "Sagacity in African Philosophy." In Serequeberhan, ed., *African Philosophy*.

Ott, Hugo. "Paths and Wrong Paths." In Neske and Kettering, eds., *Heidegger and National Socialism*.

Outlaw, Lucius. "Towards a Critical Theory of 'Race'." In Goldberg, ed., *Anatomy of Racism*.

Passmore, J. A. "The Objectivity of History." In *Conceptions of Inquiry*. Edited by Stuart Brown, John Fauvel, and Ruth Finnegan. New York: Metheun, 1981.

Searle, John. "The Battle over the University." *New York Review of Books* 37, no. 19 (Dec. 1990): 34–43.

Serequeberhan, Tsenay. "African Philosophy: The Point in Question." In Serequeberhan, ed., *African Philosophy*.

Sommers, Christina. "Where Have All the Good Deeds Gone?"; "Philosophers against the Family." In Sommers and Sommers, eds., *Vice and Virtue*.

Lévi-Strauss, Claude. "Race and History." In Kuper, ed., *Race, Science and Society*.

Theroux, Alexander. "Revenge." In Sommers and Sommers, eds., *Vice and Virtue*.

Washington, Booker T. *Up from Slavery*. In Franklin, ed., *Three Negro Classics*.

Wilhelmsen, Frederick D. "The Family as the Basis for Political Existence." *Intercollegiate Review* 26, no. 2 (Spring 1991): 9–17.

Fiction

Faulkner, William. *Light in August*. New York: Modern Library, 1968.

Johnson, James Weldon. *The Autobiography of an Ex-Colored Man*. In Franklin, ed., *Three Negro Classics*.

Morrison, Toni. *The Bluest Eye*. New York: Washington Square, 1970.

Rice, Ann. *The Feast of All Saints*. New York: Random House, 1986.

Toomer, Jean. *Cane*. New York: Liveright, 1975.

Twain, Mark. *The Tragedy of Pudd'nhead Wilson*. New York: Norton, 1980

Index

I-Pride (newsletter), 195 n.51
Irony: in Jean Toomer's life, 111;
in mixed-race literature, 131,
137–40; philosophical, 27–32

Jackson Whites (mixed-race community), 89–90
Johnson, James Weldon, 98, 101,
110, 132–33, 144
Jonas, Hans, 31

Kinney, James, 78, 128, 131
Kinship and racial designations,
19–20, 26–27
Knights of the White Camellia,
125
Ku Klux Klan, 125
Kuper, Leo, 177 n.16

Legal rulings on mixed race: in
colonies, 78–79; pre–Civil
War, 80–82; during Reconstruc-
tion, 82–83; during Revolution,
79–80. *See also* Miscegenation
laws
Leiris, Michael, 166–67
Levin, Michael, 177 n.4
Lewis, Joe, 102
Liberalism, 160–61, 165; emanci-
patory, 165–66
Liberal society and racial designa-
tions, 172
Light in August, 136–37
Ligon, Ellen Barret, 118
Line of descent, 19–20
Lloyd, Genevieve, 51
Locke, Alain, 106, 110
Locke, John, on slavery and prop-
erty, 59–61

Loving v. Virginia, 77
Lynching of blacks, 99

Marroon, etymology of, 86. *See
also* Racial islands, documented
by E. Franklin Frazier
Mencke, John G., 116. *See also*
Interracial sex
Mendelian heredity of race, 72–
73, 187 n.7
Miscegenation: believed dangers
of, 116–26; after Civil War,
83; as historical problem, 34–
36
Miscegenation laws (anti-mis-
cegenation laws), 77, 83–84.
See also Legal rulings on mixed
race
Mixed blood, false idea of, 70
Mixed race: cultural suicide of,
97–98; genocidal images of,
125–26; identification in different societies, 73–75; logical
preclusion of, 5–6; medical
prejudice, 119–20, 122–24;
neutral (theoretical) definitions
of, 73–74; statistics, 35, 126,
141; as theoretical wedge
against racism, 97
Mixed race and literature, 76,
127–28, 132–33, 137. *See also*
Faulkner, William; Hurston,
Zora Neale; Morrison, Toni;
Toomer, Nathan Eugene (Jean);
Twain, Mark
Mixed race and use of "of," 171–
72